Defeating Terrorism/Developing Dreams: Beyond 9/11 and the Iraq War

Volume One: Culture Clash / Media Demons

Volume Two: Trade Towers / War Clouds

Volume Three: Making War / Making Peace

Volume Four: In the Shadow of War

Volume Five: Turning Point:
The Rocky Road to Peace and Reconstruction

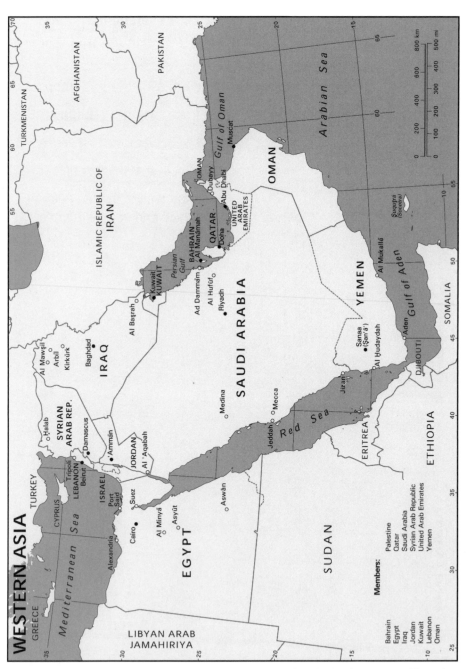

WESTERN ASIA

TURKEY

GREECE

CYPRUS

Mediterranean Sea

Ḥalab

SYRIAN
ARAB REP.

Damascus

LEBANON
Tripoli
Beirut

ISRAEL
Port
Said

ʻAmmān

JORDAN
Al ʻAqabah

Suez

Alexandria

Cairo

Al Minyā

Asyūṭ

Aswān

EGYPT

LIBYAN ARAB
JAMAHIRIYA

Al Mawṣil
Arbīl
Kirkūk

Baghdad

IRAQ

Al Baṣrah

Kuwait
KUWAIT

*Persian
Gulf*

ISLAMIC REPUBLIC OF
IRAN

AFGHANISTAN

TURKMENISTAN

PAKISTAN

Gulf of Oman

Muscat

OMAN

Dubayy
Abu Dhabi

UNITED
ARAB
EMIRATES

Arabian Sea

Suqutra
(Socotra)

BAHRAIN
Al Manāmah

QATAR
Doha

Ad Dammām

Al Hufūf

Riyadh

SAUDI ARABIA

Medina

Jeddah

Mecca

Red Sea

Jizan

Al Mukallā

YEMEN

Aden

Gulf of Aden

SOMALIA

Sanaa
(Ṣanʻāʼ)

Al Ḥudaydah

DJIBOUTI

ERITREA

ETHIOPIA

SUDAN

Members:
Bahrain
Egypt
Iraq
Kuwait
Lebanon
Oman

Palestine
Qatar
Saudi Arabia
Syrian Arab Republic
United Arab Emirates
Yemen

800 km
500 mi

© The United Nations Cartographic Section

The boundries and names shown and the designations used on this map
do not imply official endorsement or acceptance by the United Nations.

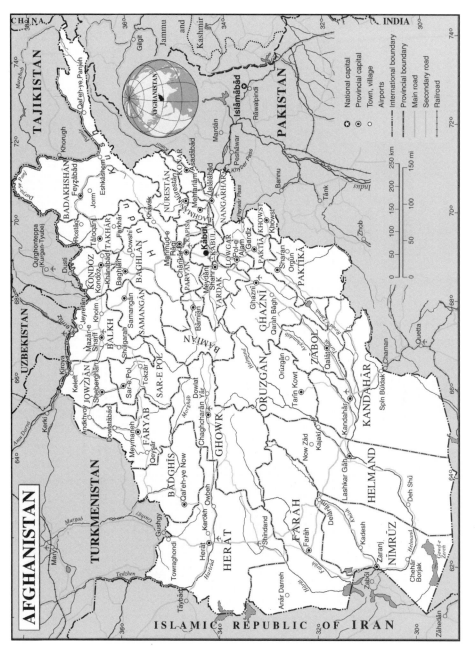

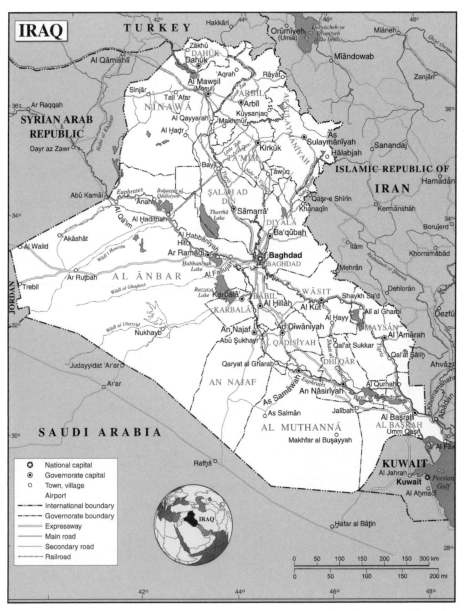

The boundaries and names shown and the designations used on this map
do not imply official endorsement or acceptance by the United Nations.

© The United Nations Cartographic Section

Defeating Terrorism/Developing Dreams:
Beyond 9/11 and the Iraq War

Volume Five

Turning Point:
The Rocky Road to Peace
and Reconstruction

Edited by Arthur B. Shostak, Ph.D.

Professor Emeritus of Sociology,
Department of Culture and Communications
Drexel University, Philadelphia, PA 19104

CHELSEA HOUSE
P U B L I S H E R S
A Haights Cross Communications Company

Philadelphia

CHELSEA HOUSE PUBLISHERS

VP, NEW PRODUCT DEVELOPMENT Sally Cheney
DIRECTOR OF PRODUCTION Kim Shinners
CREATIVE MANAGER Takeshi Takahashi
MANUFACTURING MANAGER Diann Grasse

Staff for VOLUME FIVE: TURNING POINT: THE ROCKY ROAD TO PEACE AND RECONSTRUCTION

EDITOR Christian Green
ASSISTANT EDITOR Margaret Brierton
PRODUCTION EDITOR Megan Emery
SERIES AND COVER DESIGNER Takeshi Takahashi
LAYOUT Megan Emery

http://www.chelseahouse.com

First Printing

9 8 7 6 5 4 3 2 1

Library of Congress Cataloging-in-Publication Data

Defeating terrorism : developing dreams / edited by Arthur B. Shostak.
    v. cm.
Includes bibliographical references and index.
Contents: v. 1. Culture clash : media demons — v. 2. Trade Towers :
war clouds — v. 3. Making war : making peace.
    ISBN 0-7910-7955-4 (v. 1) — ISBN 0-7910-7956-2 (v. 2) —
    ISBN 0-7910-7957-0 (v. 3) — ISBN 0-7910-7958-9 (v. 4) —
    ISBN 0-7910-8155-9 (v. 5)
1. Iraq War, 2003—Juvenile literature. 2. War on Terrorism, 2001—
Juvenile literature. 3. Terrorism—United States—Juvenile literature.
[1. Iraq War, 2003. 2. War on Terrorism, 2001- 3. Terrorism.] I.
Shostak, Arthur B. DS79.763.D44 2003 956.7044'3—dc22
                                        2003023523

■

*Dedicated to the memory of the casualties
of 9/11 and of the Iraq War ...
civilian and military alike, in the belief their sacrifice
obliges us to help leave terrorism and war behind.*

■

*Finally, it should be clear by now
that a nation can be no stronger abroad
than she is at home.*

—John F. Kennedy,
on the day of his assassination,
November 22, 1963

ACKNOWLEDGMENTS

This essay collection was the idea of Sally Cheney, the Editor-in-Chief at Chelsea House Publishers. Margaret Brierton, an Assistant Editor, has helped make enjoyable and satisfying the fast-paced process of doing five related essay volumes in the series.

Plainly, much appreciation is owed the writers of the volume's original essays, busy people who took the time to add so ably to our reflections about these remarkable times and events. One in particular, Joseph Coates, read and commented on all of the essays, a task that helped me greatly.

Anita Chiodo, a Reference Clerk at the W.W. Hagerty Library at Drexel University, located the time line material in very little time and has my gratitude; as does Alison M. Lewis, Humanities and Social Sciences Librarian at the same excellent facility.

For the past 25 years, my wife, Lynn Seng, has contributed ideas of great value, reviews of unerring accuracy, and support without which far less would be accomplished. Her belief in this project, and her love and smile, make all the difference.

Finally, I would like to acknowledge YOUR unique contribution, for it is ultimately only as you—and other readers—ponder and act on the book's many ideas that this volume can help us craft a world that increasingly honors us all.

Table of Contents

Time Line: Iraq
A Chronology of Key Events

1920   25 April—Iraq is placed under British mandate.

1921   23 August—Faysal, son of Hussein Bin Ali, the Sharif of Mecca, is crowned Iraq's first king.

1932   3 October—Iraq becomes an independent state.

1958   14 July—The monarchy is overthrown in a military coup led by Brig. Abd-al-Karim Qasim and Col. Abd-al-Salam Muhammad Arif. Iraq is declared a republic and Qasim becomes prime minister.

1963   8 February—Qasim is ousted in a coup led by the Arab Socialist Baath Party (ASBP). Arif becomes president.

1963   18 November—The Baathist government is overthrown by Arif and a group of officers.

1966   17 April—After Arif is killed in a helicopter crash on 13 April, his elder brother, Maj. Gen. Abd-al-Rahman Muhammad Arif, succeeds him as president.

1968   17 July—A Ba'thist-led coup ousts Arif and Gen. Ahmad Hasan al-Bakr becomes president.

1970   11 March—The Revolution Command Council (RCC) and Mullah Mustafa Barzani, leader of the Kurdistan Democratic Party (KDP), sign a peace agreement.

1972   A 15-year Treaty of Friendship and Cooperation is signed between Iraq and the Soviet Union.

Petroleum Firm Nationalised

1972   Iraq nationalizes the Iraq Petroleum Company (IPC).

1974   In implementation of the 1970 agreement, Iraq grants limited autonomy to the Kurds, but the KDP rejects it.

1975   March—At a meeting of the Organization of Petroleum Exporting Countries (OPEC) in Algiers, Iraq and Iran sign a treaty ending their border disputes.

1979   16 July—President al-Bakr resigns and is succeeded by Vice President Saddam Hussein.

1980   1 April—The pro-Iranian Dawah Party claims responsibility for an attack on Deputy Prime Minister, Tariq Aziz, at Mustansiriyah University, Baghdad.

Iran–Iraq War

1980   4 September—Iran shells Iraqi border towns (Iraq considers this as the start of the Iran/Iraq war). Almost one million people died in the conflict; exchanges of war dead continue.

1980   17 September—Iraq abrogates the 1975 treaty with Iran.

1980   22 September—Iraq attacks Iranian air bases.

1980   23 September—Iran bombs Iraqi military and economic targets.

1981   7 June—Israel attacks an Iraqi nuclear research centre at Tuwaythah near Baghdad.

Chemical Attack on Kurds

1988   16 March—Iraq is said to have used chemical weapons against the Kurdish town of Halabjah.

1988   20 August—A ceasefire comes into effect to be monitored by the UN Iran–Iraq Military Observer Group (UNIIMOG).

1990   15 March—Farzad Bazoft, an Iranian-born journalist with the *London Observer*, accused of spying on a military installation, is hanged in Baghdad.

Iraq Invades Kuwait

1990   2 August—Iraq invades Kuwait and is condemned by United Nations Security Council (UNSC) Resolution 660 which calls for full withdrawal.

1990   6 August—UNSC Resolution 661 imposes economic sanctions on Iraq.

1990   8 August—Iraq announces the merger of Iraq and Kuwait.

1990   29 November—UNSC Resolution 678 authorizes the states cooperating with Kuwait to use "all necessary means" to uphold UNSC Resolution 660.

1991   16–17 January—The Gulf War starts when the coalition forces begin aerial bombing of Iraq ("Operation Desert Storm"). Iraq's army was all but destroyed in the six-week conflict.

1991   13 February—U.S. planes destroy an air raid shelter at Amiriyah in Baghdad, killing more than 300 people.

1991   24 February—The start of a ground operation which results in the liberation of Kuwait on 27 February.

Ceasefire

1991   3 March—Iraq accepts the terms of a ceasefire.

1991   Mid-March/early April—Iraqi forces suppress rebellions in the south and the north of the country.

1991   8 April—A plan to establish a UN safe-haven in northern Iraq to protect the Kurds is approved at a European Union meeting. On 10 April the United States orders Iraq to end all military activity in this area.

1992   26 August—A no-fly zone, which Iraqi planes are not allowed to enter, is set up in southern Iraq, south of latitude 32 degrees north.

1993   27 June—U.S. forces launch a cruise missile attack on Iraqi intelligence headquarters in Baghdad in retaliation for the attempted assassination of U.S. President George H.W. Bush in Kuwait in April.

1994   29 May—Saddam Hussein becomes prime minister.

1994   10 November—Iraqi National Assembly recognizes Kuwait's borders and its independence.

Oil for Food

1995   14 April—UNSC Resolution 986 allows the partial resumption of Iraq's oil exports to buy food and medicine (the "oil-for-food program"). It is not accepted by Iraq until May 1996 and is not implemented until December 1996.

1995   August—Saddam Hussein's son-in-law, Gen. Hussein Kamil Hasan al-Majid, his brother, and their families leave Iraq and are granted asylum in Jordan.

1995   15 October—Saddam Hussein wins a referendum allowing him to remain president for another 7 years.

Pardoned Son-In-Law Killed

1996   20 February—Hussein Kamil Hasan al-Majid and his brother, promised a pardon by Saddam Hussein, return to Baghdad and are killed on 23 February.

1996   31 August—In response to a call for aid from the KDP, Iraqi forces launch an offensive into the northern no-fly zone and capture Irbil.

1996   3 September—U.S. extends the northern limit of the southern no-fly zone to latitude 33 degrees north, just south of Baghdad.

1996   12 December—Saddam Hussein's elder son, Uday, is seriously wounded in an assassination attempt in Baghdad.

1998   31 October—Iraq ends all forms of cooperation with the UN Special Commission to Oversee the Destruction of Iraq's Weapons of Mass Destruction (UNSCOM).

Operation Desert Fox

1998   16–19 December—After UN staff are evacuated from Baghdad, the United States and U.K. launch a bombing campaign, "Operation Desert Fox," to destroy Iraq's nuclear, chemical, and biological weapons programs.

1999   19 February—Grand Ayatollah Sayyid Muhammad Sadiq al-Sadr, spiritual leader of the Shia community, is assassinated in Najaf.

1999   17 December—UNSC Resolution 1284 creates the UN Monitoring, Verification, and Inspection Commission (UNMOVIC) to replace UNSCOM. Iraq rejects the resolution.

2000   October—Iraq resumes domestic passenger flights, the first since the 1991 Gulf War. Commercial air links re-established with Russia, Ireland, and Middle East.

2001   February—Britain, U.S. carry out bombing raids to try to disable Iraq's air defense network. The bombings have little international support.

2001   May—Saddam's son Qusay elected to the leadership of the ruling Baath Party, fuelling speculation that he's being groomed to succeed his father.

> *The light of truth belongs to us,*
> *while our enemy has the darkness of the present*
> *and the darkness of distant horizons ...*
> —Saddam Hussein TV address, January 2003

2002   April—Baghdad suspends oil exports to protest against Israeli incursions into Palestinian territories. Despite calls by Saddam Hussein, no other Arab countries follow suit. Exports resume after 30 days.

Weapons Inspectors Return

2002   September—U.S. President George W. Bush tells skeptical world leaders gathered at a UN General Assembly session to confront the "grave and gathering danger" of Iraq—or stand aside as the United States acts. In the same month British Prime Minister Tony Blair publishes a dossier on Iraq's military capability.

2002   November—UN weapons inspectors return to Iraq backed by a UN resolution which threatens serious consequences if Iraq is in "material breach" of its terms.

> *In Iraq a dictator is building and hiding weapons*
> *that could enable him to dominate the Middle East*
> *and intimidate the civilized world—*
> *and we will not allow it.*
> —U.S. President George W. Bush, February 2003

2003   March—Chief Weapons Inspector Hans Blix reports that Iraq has accelerated its cooperation but says inspectors need more time to verify Iraq's compliance.

Saddam Ousted

2003   17 March—U.K.'s ambassador to the UN says the diplomatic process on Iraq has ended; arms inspectors evacuate; U.S. President George W. Bush gives Saddam Hussein and his sons 48 hours to leave Iraq or face war.

2003   20 March—American missiles hit targets in
Baghdad, marking the start of a U.S.-led campaign
to topple Saddam Hussein. In the following days
U.S. and British ground troops enter Iraq from the
south.

2003   9 April—U.S. forces advance into central Baghdad.
Saddam Hussein's grip on the city is broken. In the
following days Kurdish fighters and U.S. forces take
control of the northern cities of Kirkuk and Mosul.
There is widespread looting in the capital and other
cities.

2003   April—U.S. lists 55 most-wanted members of former
regime in the form of a deck of cards. Former deputy
prime minister Tariq Aziz taken into custody.

2003   May—UN Security Council approves resolution
backing U.S.-led administration in Iraq and lifting of
economic sanctions. U.S. administrator abolishes Baath
Party and institutions of former regime.

2003   July—Interim governing council (IGC) meets for first
time. Commander of U.S. forces says his troops face
low-intensity guerrilla-style war. Saddam's sons Uday
and Qusay Hussein killed in gun battle at villa in
Mosul.

Guerilla Warfare Intensifies

2003   August—Bomb attack at Jordanian embassy in
Baghdad kills 11 people. Bomb attack at UN HQ in
Baghdad kills 22 people including UN's chief envoy
to Iraq. Saddam's cousin Ali Hassan al-Majid, or
Chemical Ali, captured. Car bomb in Najaf kills
125 people including Shia leader Ayatollah Mohammed
Baqr al-Hakim.

2003   September—Former chief UN weapons inspector Hans Blix says Iraq probably destroyed all its weapons of mass destruction more than a decade ago.

2003   September—A female member of the IGC dies after being shot in a gun attack in Baghdad. Aqila al-Hashimi was the only member of the former regime to be appointed to the IGC and the first IGC member to be assassinated.

2003   October—UN Security Council approves amended U.S. resolution on Iraq. The agreement gives new legitimacy to U.S.-led administration of country, but stresses power should be transferred to Iraqis "as soon as practicable."

2003   October—Dozens killed in Baghdad bombings, including attack on Red Cross office.

2003   November—Security situation continues to deteriorate. By the beginning of November—six months after President Bush declared the war officially over— more U.S. soldiers have been killed in Iraq than died during the war to oust Saddam. An Italian police base in Nasiriya is the target of a deadly suicide bomb attack.

2003   15 November—Governing Council unveils accelerated timetable for transferring country to Iraqi control.

NOTE

Material from BBC News Online
(http://news.bbc.co.uk/1/hi/world/middle_east/737483.stm)
reproduced by permission of the BBC.

Introduction

On December 3, 2003, I finished editing the manuscript for *Turning Point: The Rocky Road to Peace and Reconstruction*, the fifth volume in my ongoing series DEFEATING TERRORISM/DEVELOPING DREAMS. A few days short of the anniversary of Pearl Harbor Day, the mood seemed like what I imagined it might have been 62 years earlier after the infamous surprise attack: Both uncertainty and resolution were strong in the air. Only this much seemed clear: The U.S.-led Coalition knew a turning point had now been reached.

We found ourselves unexpectedly stymied at reforming a society wracked by decades of brutal repression and wars. A society bled by economic mismanagement and deep-seated corruption. An ersatz "nation" rift by fierce ethnic, tribal, and religious differences. Nation-building here was going to require a larger, longer, and more expensive effort (in dollars and lives) than we ever had had in mind.[1]

Many wondered if we had ever had a "Plan B?" Doubts multiplied about whether the occupation "would be effective, establishing order and preparing the way for Iraqi civilian government, or ineffective, compounding the chaos?"[2]

November, as I finished editing this volume, proved the bloodiest month yet in terms of casualties since the end of "formal hostilities." Thirty non-American troops serving as peace-keepers—men and women from Italy, Poland, Spain, and elsewhere—died, as did 81 American soldiers. (By contrast, in April, the month of the invasion, 73 Americans lost their lives.)[3] By month's end, the (little noted) number of Americans wounded during the entire campaign to date reached just over 2,000, and that included more than 1,200 hurt after major combat operations were declared over May 1.[4] Estimates of the number of Iraqi civilians killed or wounded since April 2003 ranged into the thousands, and the number of insurgents killed in combat (or as suicide bombers) will probably never be known.

This bloodshed and violence not withstanding (or, in some cases, in direct response to it), resolution hardened: For as President Bush explained—"The failure of democracy in Iraq would throw its people back into misery and turn that country over to terrorists who wish to destroy us."[5] A Gallup Poll conducted the first week of December 2003 found 59 percent of Americans thought the situation with Iraq had been worth going to war over. A majority (55 percent) thought we should keep at least the same level of troops there (this included 22 percent who wanted the number increased). Some 54 percent were confident we would be able to achieve our goals in postwar Iraq. Slightly under a majority (48 percent) thought the situation would be improved a year hence.[6]

At the same time, this same poll found a majority (56 percent) did not approve of how the United States had handled the situation with Iraq since the major fighting ended in April 2003.[7] Our "window of opportunity" was apparently closing very rapidly. At stake was not only the safety of our troops on the ground, but also whether or not we could hold the goodwill of the Iraqi people; whether or not we could put down the insurgent forces; and whether or not we could improve our strained relations with our allies, to cite just a few of many dizzying factors. Unless and until we rapidly achieved a better course of action, we seemed headed into a crisis of mind-boggling proportions.

Largely lost sight of were actual gains being made on the ground. Far more progress was being achieved than most Americans realized. Researchers, who in mid-November assessed 17 criteria, noted "encouraging trends"; "declining crime rates in Baghdad [where a third of all Iraqis live]; increasing numbers of Iraqi police officers being trained; and telephone and water services at about 80 percent of prewar levels. In addition, virtually all schools, hospitals, colleges, and courts in Iraq are now open and functioning again." Once one accepts that Iraq remains an active War Zone, "the most accurate long-term outlook is one of guarded optimism."[8]

This rare article notwithstanding, a serious imbalance in media attention and a preoccupation with vexing problems, rather than an effort at balanced coverage, helped explain costly gaps in our knowledge of the situation. Accordingly, I asked several students of postwar Iraq to tackle the toughest and most vital questions the United States faced in fall and winter 2003. Some of their essays wound up supporting, while others criticized what the U.S.-led coalition has and may yet undertake. Taken together with high-quality essays elsewhere in this five-volume series, they can help us lift the quality of our own questions, improve our tentative answers, and add value to responsible positions we take in these matters.

In part one, essayists ask: How did we get into this situation? In part two, attention is paid to major mistakes we may have made. In part three, our various accomplishments receive overdue recognition. In part four, our options are reviewed from the perspective we had at the outset of winter 2003. Finally, in the Epilogue, I briefly list some of the provocative and consequential matters we will be following from the December 3, 2003, close of this volume onto our next book in this open-ended series.

INVITATION

We look forward to regularly preparing updated editions of all the books in the series and therefore earnestly invite your thoughts, suggestions, and even offers to prepare an essay of your own. Please send all such material to Professor Art Shostak (shostaka@drexel.edu).

SUMMARY

We have much to learn from all we have been through since 9/11, the second Gulf War, our Coalition occupation of

Iraq, and the ensuing "war" to determine Iraq's fate. These experiences offer vital lessons that can help us soon forge finer lives for ourselves and for the entire world, if only we work hard and creatively at learning them. Our responsibilities here are many, and this fifth volume should help us better meet them.

FOOTNOTES

1   Reuel Marc Gerecht, "The Sabotage of Democracy," *New York Times*, 14 November 2003, A-28.
2   Harvey Sicherman, "Washington's Summer of Discontent," Foreign Policy Research Institute (www.fpri.org); 19 August 2003.
3   Edward Wong, "Forty-Six Iraqis Die in Fierce Fight Between Rebels and G.I.'s," *New York Times*, 1 December 2003, A-1.
4   Ken Dilanian, "Iraq Wounded: Ranks Swell, Unheralded," *Philadelphia Inquirer*, 23 November 2003, A-12. "A new generation of disabled veterans promises to be among the painful, expensive legacies of the Iraq war, albeit one that hasn't received much attention ... the Pentagon rarely identifies the injured, who often arrive in the United States at night and deplane out of sight of the news cameras."
5   President George W. Bush, "Bush's Words to Britons: 'Both Our Nations Serve the Cause of Freedom,'" *New York Times*, 20 November 2003, A-14.
6   David W. Moore and Joseph Carroll, "Support for U.S. Troops in Iraq Rebounds: Back to Level of Last Summer," Gallup Poll, 12 December 2003 (Gallup_Alerts@gallup.com).
7   Ibid.
8   Adriana Lins de Albuquerque, Michael O'Hanlon, and Jelly Associates, "Op-Chart." *New York Times*, 14 November 2003, A-28.

© Tim Brinton

Part One

BACKGROUND AND POSSIBILITIES

The truth is rarely pure, and never simple.
—Oscar Wilde

Our focus here is initially on some of the toughest problems of the area in general, and Iraq in particular, especially as they are exacerbated by the postwar occupation of the U.S.-led Coalition (see the sobering essay by Zaller). We look at several alternative scenarios, and weigh the rewards and costs of each. In the second essay, we explore contrasting reasons offered for initiation of the war; the varied criteria recommended for judging it a "victory"; and the many urgent domestic social needs we might remedy if we could spend here the billions we are instead spending over there, and so on (see the vexing essay by Pinto).

IRAQ: THE AFTERMATH OF INVASION AND THE FUTURE PROSPECT

Robert Zaller, Ph.D.

Professor of History and Politics,

Drexel University

Zaller's essay below calmly and clearly lays out the origins and complexities of the baffling and dangerous situation in which we find ourselves. He minces no words, and draws a stark picture of the many questions we must answer if we are soon to "bring the boys [and girls] home," and leave behind a finer Iraq and Middle East then when we struck preemptively at the Saddam Government.—Editor

---

On 19 March 2003, a U.S.-led coalition of forces, primarily American and with substantial support only from Great Britain, invaded Iraq following the failure of U.N.-brokered resolutions to give Saddam Hussein a brief additional period to disarm. Six weeks later, on 1 May, President George W. Bush declared the major part of the fighting had come to an end.

The first six months of occupation brought mixed but largely negative results. A 25-member Iraqi Governing Council (IGC), representing broad regional, tribal, and religious interests, was assembled and charged with drafting a new constitution but few resources were committed to it, and Iraq remained under a United States and British military government with no timetable for transition or withdrawal. Most prominent members of the former regime were captured or surrendered, and Saddam Hussein's two sons and presumptive successors, Uday and Qusay, were killed in a shootout, although Saddam himself remained at large until December, exhorting Iraqis to resist the occupation.

Public services such as water and power were only slowly and spottily restored, with progress hampered by persistent acts of sabotage. Oil production remained far below prewar levels, depriving Iraq of its primary source of revenue and foiling hopes within the Bush administration that the reconstruction of Iraq could largely be paid for by Iraqis themselves. Unemployment was catastrophically high, with estimates ranging from 50 to 70 percent.

The most evident problem, however, was a continuing, low-intensity war by guerrilla forces that targeted military occupiers, foreign aid workers, and Iraqi collaborators alike, as well as oil refineries and pipelines, power grids, and water systems. It appeared that these forces were a mixture of former regular army troops and militias, domestic fundamentalists, and foreign resistance fighters.

While it was unclear whether they were operating independently or partly in concert, the sophistication and effectiveness of their attacks grew as the months progressed. By mid-autumn, more American troops had been killed by these forces than had died during the invasion itself, and coalition casualties slowly but inexorably mounted.

The Bush administration was also embarrassed by its failure to find any of the so-called weapons of mass destruction it had accused Saddam Hussein of harboring and which had been cited as the primary justification for going to war. Ancillary but longer-term objectives such as promoting regional democracy and settling the Arab-Israeli conflict also suffered as resentment of the occupation grew and no apparent progress toward Iraqi self-government was made. Popular support for the occupation in Iraq itself declined to 15 percent in polls, and opposition to it grew in the United States.

In Great Britain, many believed Prime Minister Tony Blair was discredited by accusations that his government had exaggerated or distorted intelligence findings to rationalize the war. Both Britain and the United States faced the unwelcome prospect of a protracted and draining war, growing regional hostility and instability, and continued isolation from the world community.

It is difficult to make predictions about an ill-defined war against an undeclared enemy in a fractured country. Some regional as well as local consequences are already apparent, however. Popular antagonism to the United States has risen, not only in the Middle East but across the Muslim world, and the influence of fundamentalist preachers and groups is increasing.

Some of this is reflected by state toleration, if not sponsorship. The Saudi royal family has long supported radical Islamicists as a means of deflecting a potential source of resistance to its rule; while in Syria, the secular regime of Bashar al-Assad has begun to pursue a similar policy. The Pakistani military regime of Pervez Musharraf has also made concessions to militant clerics. This is worrisome for American policy, because the United States' self-proclaimed war on terrorism, while notionally supporting greater democracy, requires the policing if not the repression of Islamic fundamentalism. From this perspective, the invasion of Iraq would appear to have achieved the opposite of its objectives.

As for the future of Iraq, a suggestive if imperfect analogy can perhaps be found in the experience of the former European state of Yugoslavia. Like Iraq, Yugoslavia was established at the end of World War I in a religiously and ethnically divided region with a long tradition of intercommunal violence. As Iraq has been dominated by its Sunni religious minority, so, too, Yugoslavia was dominated by a minority ethnic and religious group, the Orthodox Serbs. Serbian control and exploitation had brought Yugoslavia to the brink of dissolution before its World War II conquest by Nazi Germany. After the war, the Communist guerrilla leader Joseph Broz Tito (1892–1980) was able to reconstruct Yugoslavia on the basis of power-sharing and political manipulation among its ethnic and religious groups, but at his death the Yugoslav federation began to fall apart, with the secessionist state of Bosnia collapsing into civil war, de facto partition, and international occupation.

Saddam Hussein did not rule by sharing power, but through a party dominated by kin and clan associates, and the Sunni religious minority. All opposition was ruthlessly crushed. Nonetheless, his brutal rule was effective in maintaining the territorial integrity of the Iraqi state, turning it into a major regional power and suppressing Islamic fundamentalism. For these reasons, and because it saw his secular regime as a bulwark against the anti-Western theocracy established in neighboring Iran by the Ayatollah Ruhollah Khomeini, the United States supported Saddam until his invasion of Kuwait in 1990. Even though gravely weakened by his defeat in the 1991 Gulf War and an ensuing regime of economic sanctions, he retained his grip over most of Iraq.

However, the northern, Kurdish third of the country became to all intents and purposes an independent entity under the cover of U.S. air power, a development that alarmed the bordering states of Turkey, Syria, and Iran, all of which possess substantial Kurdish minorities. To pursue the Balkan analogy, the support of Germany and the Vatican for the secession of the Republic of Croatia from the Yugoslav Federation in the early 1990s had similarly undermined the territorial integrity of Yugoslavia at a moment of crisis.

With the removal of Saddam from power, the Kurds remain intent on gaining the independence promised them more than 80 years ago by the Western powers, although they have refrained thus far from any attempt at overt secession and have participated in the IGC. It is certain, however, that they will insist upon genuine autonomy in any new Iraqi state and resist forcibly all but nominal control from Baghdad. This, in turn, is likely to exacerbate other regional divisions, particularly between the Shi'ite south and the so-called Sunni triangle around the capital.

There are, moreover, serious internal divisions among, as

well as between, the major ethnic and religious groups. Kurdish politics are notoriously factional, while the majority Shi'ites are divided between "moderates," who counsel patience with the American occupation until Shi'ite dominance of a new government and security from Baath loyalists can be assured, and "radicals," who insist upon an immediate American withdrawal. Sunnis, meanwhile, fear the tyranny of a Shi'ite majority, while resenting loss of the privileges that many enjoyed under Saddam.

In the absence of a military strongman of the type the United States has often preferred to unruly democracies, the Coalition Provisional Authority, led by L. Paul Bremer III, is trying to fashion a government that can somehow balance contending interests, neutralize deep suspicions, and hold age-old conflicts in check. It is trying to create, or recreate, a secular state in a country whose most popular political figures at the moment are clerics. It is attempting at least to put in place a nominal democracy where—unlike postwar Germany and Japan, examples often appealed to by the Bush administration—none has ever existed before.

Such a task would be difficult under the most ideal circumstances. In the aftermath of a destructive war, however, with a still-paralyzed economy, an ongoing war, and with little security other than that supplied by an occupying army that has had difficulty defending itself, the prospects for a stable, representative, and relatively effective civilian government are distinctly unfavorable.

If such a government cannot be formed or is unable to survive on its own, the United States will be faced with an indefinite occupation of Iraq, the necessity of finding a new strongman to replace the one it has deposed, or the still less palatable alternative of abandoning the country to civil war and, as in Yugoslavia, possible dismemberment.

As this has become apparent, the Bush administration has retreated from its initial optimism. At first, it projected a full-scale occupation of not more than a few months, with military bases remaining to replace those being phased out in Saudi

Arabia. It then contemplated a lengthier occupation, while constructing a friendly government at its leisure, only to find mounting resistance, escalating costs, and, to its dismay, difficulty in sustaining force levels even with extended tours of duty.

Now, it faces growing pressure to install a government as quickly as possible and to leave without either having pacified the country or trained an army capable of doing so. This course is clearly fraught with peril. On the other hand, U.S. presence itself has been destabilizing, and the longer it stays, the likelier it is that whatever regime it leaves behind will be perceived as compromised. There are no attractive options.

U.S. policymakers saw a post-Saddam Iraq as the key to a new Middle East. With Iraq in hand, Iran, the last remaining independent power of consequence in the region, would be isolated. A friendly regime in Baghdad would give the United States further leverage on Saudi Arabia, with its vast oil reserves and its covert patronage of terrorism. An Arab-Israeli settlement could be dictated and the Muslim world made safe for capitalism and democracy.

Those who entertained this grandiose vision may have been right on one point: Iraq could well be the key to the future of the Middle East. If, however, the U.S. invasion of Iraq produces a Vietnam-style quagmire or civil anarchy instead of a secular, pro-Western regime, the entire region could be thrown into turmoil, with unpredictable consequences for an oil-dependent world economy. This, too, may be an extreme scenario, but the risks of such an outcome are undeniably present. Prudence would have dictated that these factors be considered before American bombs began to fall.

■ Essay Two ■

IRAQ—NO FAIRY-TALE ENDING

Jim Pinto

Member of the Association of Professional Futurists
and the World Future Society

Pinto's essay below raises a host of nettle-some questions and challenges us to find answers that are less than obvious, more nuanced than common, and as constructive as possible. He reminds us, for example, of lingering questions we have about the competence of a U.S. intelligence establishment that could not decide whether or not Saddam had weapons of mass destruction. He asks if we had sound plans on hand for the aftermath of the six-week war, and if not, why not? He reviews four major reasons for the war, the criteria by which to assess our "victory," alternative ways we might spend the $87 billion being pumped into Iraq this year alone, and, finally, what YOU and I might do about any of this.—Editor

---

On May 1, 2003, just weeks after the war in Iraq had commenced, the world was treated to an unusual spectacle, a fairy-tale ending. Dressed in a top-gun outfit, the victorious U.S. Commander-in-Chief made a spectacular landing on an aircraft carrier to speak to the troops. The banner behind him announced, "Mission Accomplished!" And he proclaimed victory, "We have prevailed!" Apparently, this was Vice President Dick Cheney's "brilliant" public-relations idea, which many protested as a blatant photo-op backdrop for the coming presidential campaign.

Had that really been the end of the war with Iraq, the images may have been remembered as a triumph of American superiority. But the war lingered, and U.S. soldiers continue to be killed at an average of one or two a day, sometimes more, with sudden deadly spurts of resistance. Within just a few months, more U.S. troops had been killed after the supposed end of the war than since the start. And, still, there is no respite. When resistance erupted, President Bush proclaimed with juvenile bravado, "Bring 'em on!" And when the killing continued with repugnant regularity, he repeated his empty rhetoric, "We will not run!"

NO REAL JUSTIFICATION FOR WAR

President Bush has a serious problem. When he asked Congress to authorize use of American military forces in Iraq, he made a number of unequivocal statements to justify a preemptive war. Now many of his statements appear to be false. U.S. intelligence was reporting that there was no direct evidence of Weapons of Mass Destruction (WMD). Bush launched the war anyway.

Almost a year after the war with Iraq supposedly ended, there is still no evidence of WMD, and the international community views the United States with suspicion and even fear. Respected U.S. news magazines like *Newsweek* and *Time* reported that some WMD evidence was faked and U.S. intelligence was ignored. But President Bush keeps insisting that Iraq has WMD and the war was justified.

THE REAL REASONS FOR THE WAR WITH IRAQ

New York Times columnist Tom Friedman, who has spent a great deal of time in the Middle East and understands the complex situation, suggests there were actually four reasons for the war: the real reason, the right reason, the moral reason, and the stated reason.[1]

The "real reason" was that after 9/11 the United States needed to hit someone in the Arab-Muslim world. Afghanistan wasn't enough. We hit Saddam because we could, because he deserved it, and because he was in the heart of that world. And every neighboring government got the message: "Don't mess with the U.S.!"

The "right reason" was the need to partner with Iraqis, post-Saddam, to build a new, progressive Arab regime. The real threats are not WMD but the growing number of angry, humiliated young Arabs and Muslims who hate the United States more than anything. Helping to build a new Iraq as a model for others and solving the Israeli-Palestinian conflict are necessary steps in defusing the *ideas* of mass destruction, which are what really threaten us.

The "moral reason" for the war was that Saddam's regime was a catalyst for mass destruction and genocide that had killed thousands of his own people, and neighbors, and needed to be stopped. We have demonstrated that this reason was indeed justified.

Somehow, the Bush administration felt that it could never win support for the right reasons and the moral reasons. So, it opted for the "stated reason": Saddam had weapons of mass destruction that posed an immediate threat to the United States. If it turns out that the evidence for WMDs was fabricated, the image of the United States could be greatly damaged.

Finding Iraq's WMDs is necessary to preserve the credibility of the Bush team, but rebuilding Iraq is necessary to win the real war, because the future of the Middle East rides on a new Iraq. That will take time.

SUCCESS CRITERIA

The war with Iraq is a historical fact. Where will it lead? Was the significant U.S. commitment worth what it has already cost and continues to demand?

In April 2003, Friedman listed the criteria by which the world could judge whether the United States had indeed "won" the war.[2] I have summarized the criteria here and expanded them to include updates from a half-year later.

1. *Has the United States occupied Baghdad—without leveling the whole city?*
   Yes.

2. *Have we killed, captured, or expelled Saddam?*
   Not killed but certainly removed from power and captured.

3. *Have we explained why we haven't been "greeted with garlands," as expected?*
   While many Iraqis seem to welcome the regime change, clearly most still consider this to be an invasion and the United States to be an occupying force. Happily, free speech has returned; but sadly, previously exiled clerical leaders are exercising their right to inflame the masses.

4. *Have we found any weapons of mass destruction?*
   While the United States still stubbornly keeps looking, most of the world has concluded that there are no WMD in Iraq. The path is being prepared to admit that perhaps nothing will be found "for a long time," but "it doesn't really matter because Saddam was clearly evil anyway."

5. *Have any links with bin Laden and al Qaeda been found?*
   The Bush administration clearly implied that there were indeed links with al Qaeda and terrorism, but President Bush himself admitted in October 2003 that there were no direct links.

6. *Has the territorial integrity of Iraq been preserved?*
   Yes.

7. *Has an authentic nationalist Iraqi emerged to lead Iraq?*
   Not yet.

8. *Is the Iraqi state that emerges from this war legitimately accepted by Iraq's Arab and Muslim neighbors?*
   It remains to be seen.

WHAT NEXT?

Clearly the United States must take the responsibility to rebuild Iraq into a progressive, democratic model that works. The occupation could last years, cost many billions of dollars, and involve tens of thousands of occupying troops. Bungled UN diplomacy means that the United States will bear most of the financial burden. But with its current economic woes the United States probably does not have the stomach, or the stamina, for taking on the responsibility of rebuilding a country of 26 million people, half a world away. And this even before U.S. involvement in Afghanistan is complete.

After previously snubbing the UN, the United States offered the Security Council a resolution calling for the elimination of more international sanctions on Iraq and granting the United States broad control over the country's oil industry and revenue until a permanent, representative Iraqi government can be put into place. The United States seemed to request UN approval for control that it had already seized with force. And with peculiar pride, financial aid and military assistance were proposed without giving up any control whatsoever. It was no surprise that all major UN members declined to help, refusing to approve a resolution that was only empty rhetoric.

In the meantime, already saddled with an all-time record U.S. budget deficit approaching $500 billion and high domestic unemployment, Congress reluctantly approved an additional $87 billion for the coming year of which $67 billion was allocated to support U.S. troops in the area. With 140,000 U.S. troops now in Iraq, the Bush administration admits that a similar number will likely remain a year hence.

The balance of the $20 billion would be used to finance the construction of Iraq's infrastructure. There was some discussion about making the $20 billion a loan, but that was dismissed as ineffective and futile. So, the money has been approved, with no foreseeable end to U.S. involvement in

Iraq in sight—short of a transfer of power to the world community through the UN. Perhaps only a new president will be willing and able to implement such a plan.

WHAT WOULD $87 BILLION BUY?

This year, the U.S. budget deficit has climbed to nearly $500 billion—about 5 percent of the gross domestic product (GDP). That is more than the GDP of all but 17 countries in the world. The recent tax cut will cost the federal government about $300 billion this year alone. In addition, Congress is now considering whether to spend $87 billion in Iraq. That's not a loan—it's a "grant," paid by U.S. taxpayers. To bring some perspective to the $87 billion, which is more than the GDP of all but 40 countries in the world, *Newsweek* has proposed what the federal government might do in other key policy areas if it had $87 billion lying around.

Here are some real-life examples of what $87 billion equates to:

- More than the combined total of all U.S. state budget deficits.
- Two years worth of all U.S. unemployment benefits; enough to pay the 3.3 million people who have lost their jobs (since President Bush took office) $26,363 each.
- More than double the total budget for Homeland Security.
- 87 times the amount the government spends on after-school programs.
- More than 10 times the amount the government spends on environmental protection.
- 58 times the proposed federal funding for community health centers.
- Could hire more than 2 million new teachers, police officers, or firefighters nationwide.

9/11 ANNIVERSARY THOUGHTS

As the somber second anniversary of 9/11 has come and gone, let's stop to think about what is happening here. In the words of Buffalo Springfield's 1967 song, "For What It's Worth":

There's somethin' happening here,
What it is ain't exactly clear.
There's a man with a gun over there,
Tellin' me I gotta beware.
I think it's time we stop,
Hey, what's that sound?
Everybody look what's going down.

The world changed forever on 9/11. Two years after, the date again gave us pause. There's something happenin' here.

Have we caught Osama bin Laden, the archvillain behind the atrocity? No. Instead we went out and subdued Afghanistan, one of the poorest countries in the world. Yet bin Laden and the Taliban are still there. Just recently his new video tape warned of more terror.

Have we caught the anthrax killer, who supposedly had the same evil intentions? No, we've kinda forgotten that. Instead, ever obedient to the president's personal obsession, we went after Saddam Hussein and occupied Iraq.

We were told that Saddam had WMD. Will we ever find the WMD? Not likely. The rhetoric has now shifted to "WMD programs" and even those references have almost disappeared.

Despite the brevity of the war with Iraq, 139 U.S. troops were killed. Unfortunately, more than that number have died since, with even more casualties mounting almost every day. Disgracefully, no one even speaks about the number of dead Iraqis, estimated at over 10,000. Similarly, little was ever said about more than 2,000,000 dead Vietnamese.

The United States chose to attack Iraq and terror attacks now occur there because we are there. What was sold to Congress and the U.S. public as WMD and freedom for the Iraqi people is now being resold as "the central war on terror." Should we believe that we are somehow safer now?

It is more than two years later. Has the risk of terrorism increased, or decreased, because of Afghanistan and Iraq? President Hosni Mubarak of Egypt warned: "The war in Iraq will create hundreds more bin Ladens!" Has it?

Democracy means that the buck ultimately stops with us, the voters. We must face facts, accept personal responsibility, and do whatever we can as individual citizens. Now is the time.

Here is what YOU can do:

• Write letters and e-mails to newspapers and news magazines.
• Use the Internet to circulate your own ideas and opinions.
• Question candidates for office about their specific ideas on Iraq, and what they think of the $87 billion the United States has budgeted for Iraq this year. You can do this by visiting their Web sites and using their feedback links.
• Engage your parents, relatives, friends, and neighbors in extended and constructive dialogue about our challenge in Iraq and the Middle East. Listen, and express your own opinion.

FOOTNOTES

1 Tom Friedman, "Because We Could," *New York Times*, 4 June 2003.
2 Tom Friedman, "Scorecard for the War," *New York Times*, 30 March 2003.

12-15-03 THE PHILADELPHIA INQUIRER. UNIVERSAL PRESS SYNDICATE.

Part Two

WHAT WENT WRONG—AND WHY?

I am driven by many things. I know what some of them are. The misery that people suffer and the misery for which I share responsibility. That is agonizing. We live in a free society, and privilege confers responsibility....
—Noam Chomsky

Good intentions not withstanding, in late fall 2003, the "Iraqification" of the security forces had not dimmed the rate or deadliness of attacks against coalition troops. The Iraqi Governing Council and various leading clerics were willfully stalling the process of drafting a new constitution. And polling indicated more and more Iraqis were disappointed with, and even angry at, the American presence.

The section's first essay helps explain much of the downward spiral by highlighting the explanatory value here of *culture*. Ours, for example, is an individualistic culture; that of the Iraqis, a collectivistic one, and this makes all the difference in the world! Once we take the two very different worldviews carefully into account, many of our post-War heartaches in Iraq "make sense," and we can begin to see our way beyond them (see the instructive essay by Nikolaev).

The second essay also employs the concept of culture, though indirectly: It applies to our Iraq experience the "test" of 12 adages, 12 pieces of "wisdom," such as the notion that *one should look before one leaps*. Did our leaders do that? That is, was the invasion of Iraq preceded by the quality of planning and preparation such an enormous undertaking would seem to merit? Held against this novel test of sorts, the entire Iraq campaign does not come off well, thereby suggesting much that can be learned for our advantage (see the sage essay by Coates).

43

ARE MORAL JUSTIFICATIONS FOR WAR REALLY MORAL?

Alexander G. Nikolaev, Ph.D.

Assistant Professor of Communication,
Drexel University

Culture makes an extraordinary difference and we overlook its significance at great peril— as when our troops are not given lessons in Iraqi cultural ways before arriving in that country. Ours is an individualistic culture; theirs, a collectivistic one, and the essay below explains why this far-reaching difference explains a lot about our problems in the Middle East. Unless and until we get more sophisticated about cultural differences, we will continue to make unnecessary, unbecoming, and even mortally dangerous mistakes.—Editor

---

One of the main consequences of the 2003 War in Iraq is that it is highly likely that it will be used as justification for other wars in the future.[1] A romantic myth of liberation is very attractive to American people, who may ask in the future: "If we did it so successfully in Iraq, why can't we do it in North Korea, Syria, or Iran?" As it is now clear the Weapons of Mass Destruction story was a hoax, a moral justification for war would seem one especially good way to justify the Iraq misadventure.

President Bush reiterated that "the values of our country

lead us to confront this gathering threat." (Bush Calls on Americans, 2002). In the State of the Union Address on January 29, 2002, Bush also emphasized that "America will always stand firm for the non-negotiable demands of human dignity; rule of law; limits on the power of the state; respect for women; private property; free speech; equal justice; and religious tolerance." But probably the strongest statement he made was during his West Point Address on June 3, 2002: "Moral truth is the same in every culture, in every time, and in every place. We are in conflict between good and evil, and America will call evil by its name."

The problem is that moral truth is *not* the same in every culture, in every time, and in every place. What Mr. Bush and people like him do not understand is that all these words are labels. And every culture and nation can have different meanings for these labels. What is freedom for an American is not necessarily that for a Russian, Chinese, or Arab.

Let's go over just some of these labels and see how differently they can be perceived and understood by different nations and cultures.

FREEDOM

The concept of *freedom* is probably the most controversial and misunderstood. Americans interpret freedom as the ability of each individual to do whatever he or she deems appropriate and necessary in every situation of life. Therefore, American culture is categorized as the *quintessential individualistic* culture. But Arab cultures, for example, have a different view—one that is *collectivistic*. Members of this type of culture believe every person can be free only when the society as a whole is free— free from fear, exploitation, and injustice.

In the American culture, people are valued for their ability to overcome their problems and individual shortcomings and succeed *almost* regardless of what barriers stand in their way. In collectivistic cultures, people are not supposed to overcome anything—it is the main task of society to make sure that no unfortunate problem or even individual inadequacy ruin a human life. Society as a whole is responsible for the success or failure of its members. Many Arab countries subscribe to this cultural approach, especially Iraq.

Members of collectivistic cultures believe *real* freedom is the freedom of the society as a whole to keep thieves and killers in check, and, by so doing, to provide each citizen of this society freedom from fear, oppression, and injustice. Many people from collectivistic cultures would say (and I have personally heard it many times) that the freedom of the individual—which is the prime focus of individualistic cultures—is reduced to the freedom for each person to kill and steal if he or she deems it appropriate in a certain life situation. That is why "individualist" is a swear word in collectivistic societies.

Iraq was and remains a collectivistic culture. And the criminal frenzy that followed the fall of Baghdad again proved to many Iraqis that in their cultural environment the individualistic (or American) notion of freedom is *not* going to work.

FREEDOM OF SPEECH

What is puzzling for many people in the world is when Americans equate the ideas of free speech, free media, and private media. How can a journalist be free from a person who signs his or her paycheck and can fire him or her at any time? How can NBC journalists disagree with the war in Iraq when NBC is owned by General Electric—one of the largest military contractors in the country? GE needs this war, so does NBC. Therefore, journalists may be scared to disagree with what they are told to say on the air. (Besides that, all journalists are carefully selected, indoctrinated, trained, and matched with their assignments to help assure that they will provide the "right" coverage for their audience.)

That is why many countries maintain a substantial system of state-owned or state-supported media channels. They believe that truth, fairness, and objectivity are too important to be left to private interests. Many of them believe that the presence of private media controlled and owned by foreigners amounts to foreign brain control and intellectual occupation of their countries (many so-called "free media" outlets are indeed controlled and run by the CIA, such as Radio Liberty, Radio Free Europe, etc.) Therefore, we should not be astonished when people in other countries resist our efforts to bring them "free" media and freedom of speech—according to *our* standards.

This helps explain why many Iraqis are not in a hurry to establish private media. Most media organizations in the Arab world are either government-owned or government-supported. In this form they are more credible to many members of the collectivistic culture and any effort to impose "free media" on them will probably initially fail.

DEMOCRACY AND CAPITALISM

As for democracy, it means respect for the power of all people. But under the American election system—where the winner takes all—the right of the minority may be disregarded. Many countries consider this system undemocratic and prefer to have decisions made either by consensus (as at the United Nations) or by compromise.

Secondly, private media take money for their services. Therefore, in order to be known and to be elected one must have millions of dollars. This means that only rich people or those who serve the rich can readily get elected. Under this system, the poor have no say in the political decision-making process. In other countries (such as Scandinavian countries, Netherlands, Germany, France, or Japan) election laws strictly limit the role of money in the election process, provide for equal media coverage, and make many other provisions to ensure the fairness of the electoral process. The rules created in the United States to police this process are mostly symbolic and can be avoided through many legal loopholes.

In a similar way, Iraqis will never vote for a "TV-based candidate": a person they don't know but just saw on TV in a commercial. They vote for so-called opinion leaders (as in any collectivistic culture). These people may be religious leaders, scientists, cultural leaders, well-known established politicians, elders, or tribal leaders. But even they have to rule in a collective manner—through a national council or representative body. The supreme ruler is usually chosen by such a council based on his experience and political skills, not simply on slogans that can deceive people.

This is a very ancient and wise system that evolved over thousands of years, and it is best suited for this particular culture. Unfortunately, Iraq has spent the last several hundred years under colonial rule, and it did not have a chance to fully develop and enjoy its own ancient system. Therefore, many Iraqis intend to see they are not denied this opportunity again.

The same can be said about the best version of capitalism for Iraq. Many proponents of cultural universalism would say that the United States brings other people democracy and capitalism and the whole world is moving in that direction.

What most Americans don't know is that there are *different* types of capitalism. European and some Asian countries are practicing the *Rhine* model (Albert, 1991; Marshal and Tucker, 1992; Sennett, 1998), which proposes social responsibility, provides a number of social guaranties, and strongly regulates private entrepreneurship. This system also provides free health care and education. (The Russians, for example, tried the American system, and are now trying to transform it into something far more similar to the European Rhine model).

The United States is the only industrialized country that does not provide free health care and education for all its citizens. Some people would say there is not enough money for this. But the example set by other industrialized countries challenges this statement. Government just has to know how to manage money differently ... and many Iraqis intend to do so.

On September 23, 2003, CNN's Walter Rodgers reported that, according to a study conducted in Iraq, the two things Iraqis fear the most in the future are the privatization of their health care system and the institution of fees for higher education. This shows they are not afraid of capitalism as such but rather of having the U.S. market-driven model imposed on them.

DO WE HAVE A RIGHT TO IMPOSE OUR VALUES
AND IDEAS ONTO OTHERS?

Any notion that American ideas and values are universally accepted is mistaken. If, let's say, some ruling authority came to this country and tried to make our women wear chadors, Americans would have refused and resisted (especially if it had been done by force). Why are we amazed when other people resist the imposition of our values on them?

It is impossible to take one set of moral values and apply them to other people without threatening the way of life they have created over thousands of years; one that fits their needs and ideas best, and helps them survive in their physical and social environment. By applying our moral standards to them, we may threaten their very survival; and many will fight to the death for their survival.

Our system works for us because we created it according to our needs and standards. This system has evolved in our country over hundreds of years. We know how to live in this system, how to survive, how to use it to our advantage, how to get the most out of it; and, by and large, we like much about it. We do not want anybody to come here and undermine it. Why then do we think we can go elsewhere and change the system of others?

For many years we fought the Communists because we were told that they wanted to spread their ideology by force. How will we be different if we promote our ideology in that way? No wonder certain people fight us with the same fierce determination with which we fought the Communists.

If and when we feel ready to try to help others around the world we should remain wary of using "moral reasoning." Moral standards vary greatly from culture to culture, and the whole moral rhetoric is commonly used as a smoke screen to hide other self-serving reasons for going to war.

What we should do is break out of the shell of egocentrism, propaganda, and deceit. Instead, we should look around us—around the world—at how other nations *really* live. We are not going to adopt many of their moral standards because they may not be right for us. But this recognition of their way of life will help us to live in peace with other cultures. Instead of urging or even forcing our imperfections on other people, we have to first improve our own democracy and our own lives.

FOOTNOTE

1   The 1999 war in Kosovo was used as a moral justification for the 2003 Iraq War ("If we were able to bring democracy and freedom to Kosovo, why won't we do it in Iraq?") Make no mistake: the 1999 war in Kosovo had absolutely disastrous consequences for the population of that small Serbian province. Ironically, the terrorists who now rule Kosovo, under the protection of mostly American forces, are a part of the al Qaeda network and were organized, armed, and trained by Osama bin Laden himself. (U.S. Senate Republican Policy Committee, 1999; Human Rights Watch, 2001; Copley, 1999).

REFERENCES

Albert, Michael. *Capitalism against Capitalism*. London: Whurr, 1993.
Bush Calls on Americans to Support Strong Steps against Iraq. (7 October 2002). [Electronic file]. *The U.S. Department of State International Information Programs*. Available at <http://usinfo.state.gov/regional/nea/iraq/text/1007bhamer.htm>.
Copley, Gregory R., ed. The New Rome & the New Religious Wars. Defense & Foreign Affairs Washington, D.C.: The International Strategic Studies Association, 1999. Available at <www.strategicstudies.org/crisis/newrome.htm>.
Human Rights Watch. *Kosovo*. Available at <www.hrw.org/reports/2001/kosovo/Iraqbodycount.net.> (10 August 2003). Available at <www.iraqbodycount.net>.
Marshal, Ray and Marc Tucker. *Thinking for a living: Education and the Wealth of Nations*. New York: Harper Collins, 1992.
Sennett, Richard. *The Corrosion of Character: The Personal Consequences of Work in the New Capitalism*. New York: W.W. Norton & Company, 1998.

The State of the Union Address by President George W. Bush. (29 January 2002). [Electronic file]. *Bushcountry.org.* Available at <http://www.bushcountry.org/bush_speeches/ president_bush_speech_012902.htm>.

U.S. Senate Republican Policy Committee. (March 1999). *The Kosovo Liberation Army: Does Clinton Policy Support Group with Terror, Drug Ties? From 'terrorists' to 'partners'* Available at <www.senate.gov/~rpc/releases/1999/fr033199.htm>.

West Point Address by President George W. Bush. (3 June 2002). [Electronic file]. *NewsMax.com* Available at <http://www.newsmax.com/archives/artcles/2002/6/2/81009.shtm>.

■ Essay Four ■

NO AFTERMATH TO IRAQ YET

Joseph F. Coates

President, Joseph F. Coates Consulting Futurist, Inc.

The remarkably fresh, novel, and sagacious essay below takes "a dozen widely, if not universally accepted beliefs about human behavior, and then [fits] the events in Iraq into violations of, ignorance of, or underuse of those general precepts." Read carefully and savored, the essay has much to teach about why so many problems haunt the postwar scene in Iraq, as well as in our lives in general. Better still, the essay points the way to many pragmatic improvements we might make over there and here as well—both in public and private matters.—Editor

---

It was November 1, 2003, when I began this essay. The original plan was to pull together—some six months after the end of the conflict—the military, social, political, economic, and other developments in Iraq concerning liberation, rehabilitation, reform, and reconstruction. That is not practical now, because the conflict is far from over. Some presumably small groups of Iraqis, close adherents to Saddam Hussein and aided by an indeterminate number of outsiders, are now engaged in destructive and deadly actions against U.S. armed forces and civilian personnel; representatives of international agencies in Iraq; and local people, including police, who are cooperating with U.S. and allied forces.

Iraq is politically divided along ethnic, religious, and ideological lines. Some religious groups, as well as others, are vociferously opposed to the continued presence of U.S. troops. They feel, in a strongly nationalistic way, that the Americans should get out and let them settle their own affairs. Other small groups use instances in which Iraqis are killed, injured, or dislocated by American troops as a rallying cry.

To pursue all the details in the last six months of development and their origins, consequences, and reactions, is premature. It's a job for historians and a story that is not likely to be accurately told in the next ten years. The assignment of responsibility, and hence of blame, is premature and too politically charged now to be useful.

Rather than pursue those lines, I've chosen to present a dozen widely, if not universally, accepted beliefs about human behavior, and then fit the events in Iraq into violations of, ignorance of, or underuse of those general precepts.

1. LOOK BEFORE YOU LEAP

Aesop's Fables, which are widely viewed in the Western world as sensible guides to human behavior, include the tale of the fox who finds himself in a well. He hails a passing goat, tells him how great the water is, and convinces the goat that he should jump in. The fox then points out that they are stuck. There is no obvious way to get out. He then comes up with a bright idea. He has the goat stand on his hind legs and lean against the wall. The fox promises to run up his back to reach the rim and then help the goat to get out. Of course the fox gets out and does not help the goat. When the goat complains, the fox dismisses him as, "You foolish old fellow." The lesson is "look before you leap."

The United States was obviously unprepared for the limited enthusiasm the Iraqi people displayed after they were liberated, the destructive behavior of those who began to vandalize and loot buildings and offices, and those who even attacked the most important assets of the country, assets which could provide Iraq with international income, namely, the oil wells and pipelines.

2. ALWAYS HAVE AN EXIT STRATEGY

Positively linked to Aesop's fable is the military's core belief that every action should be associated with a preplanned exit strategy; that is, when planning to get into a situation, one should know how to get out and have a specific strategy for getting out.

It is worth noting the difference between tactics and strategies. Tactics are the moment-to-moment, day-to-day plans and operations of the military. Strategy is the overall grand plan that allows the military to deal tactically with expected, as well as unexpected, events.

There appears to be no exit strategy from Iraq. There is no publicly presented definition of when it will be time for the United States to move out, the conditions for moving out, or for that matter what moving out would mean. Would it mean an end to all aid and help or only military aid?

In the absence of an exit strategy, it is difficult to have a perspective on how long the continuing hostilities will last and at what point we would be able to remove ourselves. Whether it is months, years, or decades; at the moment the question is an open befuddling one that makes many people unhappy, anxious, or alarmed about the total future cost in material and lives. Remember, Aesop's goat had no exit strategy.

3. WIELD OCCAM'S RAZOR

William of Occam, who lived in the late thirteenth and early fourteenth centuries, was an English philosopher who is most famous for what is now known as "Occam's Razor." It was a point in his argument, logic, and rhetoric that the more things you mention as a cause, that is, as a source of some situation, the less credible your argument is. His principle was "Do not multiply entities beyond necessity." The more complex your story, the more difficult it is for you to sustain it and for others to believe it.

We now see that the numerous reasons for entering Iraq, presented one after another before we moved in, are unsustainable by postinvasion evidence. First, Iraq was loosely linked to the terrorists responsible for the events of 9/11, that is, the destruction of the Twin Towers in New York and the fact that al Qaeda fighters found refuge and succor in Iraq. The facts after the invasion do not support either claim.

There was the point that Iraq was engaged in producing nuclear weapons. After six months of on-the-ground searching by the United States, the unequivocal outcome is that there was no nuclear weapons program in Iraq in the past decade.

Then there was the claim that Iraq had both chemical and biological warfare capabilities, and that these weapons could be launched very, very quickly. No tangible evidence has been found of any significant capability with regard to either of these classes of weapons of mass destruction. The best testimony from the Iraqis, who ostensibly would know about such weapons, is that those programs were dropped years ago.

The consequence of having multiple reasons for invading Iraq rapidly loses all credibility as each one is proved to have been a chimera, that is, a nonexistent fantasy.

4. THE IDEOLOGUE HAS THE ANSWER EVEN BEFORE UNDERSTANDING THE QUESTION

Merriam-Webster's Collegiate Dictionary gives four closely linked definitions of ideology: 1) Visionary theorizing; 2a) A systematic body of concepts, esp. about human life or culture; 2b) a manner or the content of thinking characteristic of an individual, group, or culture; 2c) the integrated assertions, series and aims that constitute a sociopolitical program.

The key characteristic of an ideologue, that is, an adherent to an ideology whether it be Marxism, communism, socialism, Buddhism, Confucianism, Taoism, vegetarianism, etc., is that he or she knows the answer even before understanding the question. The ideologue's vision is rigid and inflexible. Fixed explanations for situations one does not like, coupled with formula solutions, do not provide a basis for fresh understanding of new situations or solutions tailored to special conditions.

The United States has seriously stumbled over its ideological preconceptions in Iraq from beginning to end. For one thing, we have repeatedly been told that we are bringing free markets and democracy, the inevitable link to free markets, to the people of Iraq. By no means is there universal or even consensus agreement among scholars that the free market is a necessary correlate or accompaniment to democracy, or vice versa. Rather, it represents one ideological point of view, which is now to a substantial degree dominant in the U.S. government and widely celebrated in business.

The reality in Islamic countries is that democracy and the way it is developed in Western Europe, particularly in the Anglo-Saxon countries, is alien to the traditions of Islamic life. Islamic political life is characterized in two ways: One is that governance must be intimately tied to religious beliefs, in sharp contrast to our American belief in the absolute separation of church and state. Second, religious beliefs must play a crucial role in that government. In much of Islam, there are religious courts that perform many of the duties that we in the West have assigned to strictly secular courts. The religious court's framework is hundreds of years old. They often mete out punishments grossly offensive to Western values and in violation of the United Nations' stance on human rights.

The notion that free markets and democracy are inextricably linked is a historic error further compounded by the confusion as to what exactly a free market is. Does it mean no holds barred, all-out conflict between and among buyers and sellers? Does it mean inevitable growth of global corporations? Does it mean universal access at fair prices to goods everywhere? Is it antimonopolistic or promonopolistic? The ideology underlying one of our objectives in Iraq is founded on political misunderstanding and dubious economic precepts.

The incongruity, if not outright contradictions, between American ideology, and local customs and universal beliefs, may create a wide chasm to be spanned by the council set up to lay the basis for democratic voting, and a new Western-Islamic hybrid constitution. An imposed American ideology of one man, one vote is antithetical to Iraqi thinking in which a clan, the tribe, and the religious group to which one belongs are one's primary affiliations.

In a society organized around tribes, the concept of one man, one vote leaves open the terrible possibility that, once the majority takes power, it becomes their opportunity to "get even." The flexibility and regard for the rightful and fair treatment of every citizen in a democracy may be terribly thwarted when the Iraqi electorate goes into the voting booth.

Inversion of an old expression "I'll believe it when I see it" finds its own value among ideologues: "I'll see it when I believe it." This shows up in different ways in the Iraq situation. First was the incorrect overemphasis on Iraq as a refuge or base for terrorists. Al Qaeda and the Taliban in Afghanistan were primarily motivated by a need to reform Islam and reestablish traditional values. Iraq as a secular state would hardly be the place where one would expect them to find assistance. As it turns out, they were not in Iraq. Whether, more recently, former and would-be terrorists are finding an opportunity to get back at the United States by assisting dissident groups in Iraq is an open question.

Ideology can even affect well-established organizational behavior. Before we went into Iraq, Secretary of Defense Donald Rumsfeld had a legitimate objective of moving the three armed services, the Army, Navy, and Air Force, into high-tech based services and to rely more on the use of special forces in future combat. He has been quite successful with the Navy and Air Force, but has met consistent resistance from the Army brass.

For example, before we invaded Iraq, the Army argued that at least a quarter-million men would be necessary not just to achieve victory but to hold the terrain until we accomplished what was needed in the postconflict period. The secretary pooh-poohed the Army's position because he thought he knew better.

By providing fewer troops than the Army knew it needed, we now see some of the consequences: early on, looting of national treasures in museums and destruction of infrastructure; and, most recently, the discovery of hundreds of weapons caches and perhaps a million tons of armaments, so numerous that U.S. forces cannot adequately guard them. That makes them attractive sites for virtually anyone in Iraq to steal weapons for later use; in many cases, for later use against Americans or for export to insurgent groups.

The secretary's belief that the reorganized military would be able to defeat the enemy forced the Army to rely on high-tech and special forces. The secretary's view seems to be borne out in the formal military encounters in Iraq that were responsible for achieving victory in 23 days. However, his single-minded ideology overlooked what it would take to occupy the country in order to establish a new era of reform. The special forces were untrained and unprepared to deal with civilians in a civilian context. As a result, we see a continual round of reported incidents, since the occupation, of culture clashes between local people and the foreign troops who haven't the foggiest idea of the cultural differences that they encounter and have to deal with daily.

Other consequences of the ideological approach and of Americans' self-righteousness, discussed below, were to fail to anticipate the gross shift in world opinion resulting from this country's unilateral invasion, contrary to the expressed wishes of the United Nations. Favorable opinions of the United States in public opinion polls in a dozen or more large and small countries have dropped anywhere from 10 to 50 percent. Countries that would never have dreamt of being at risk of an invasion by the United States, or an occupation, are now fearful. The objective validity of those fears is not the point. Our actions created an image and that image shifts public opinion.

Almost surely another unanticipated effect of the unilateral movement into Iraq was to mobilize a Pan-Islamic view against the United States, and make already existing doubts and hostilities toward the United States more certain. Iraq is an Islamic country. Our unilateral move, with incidental support from the United Kingdom and small levels of support from other countries, focuses attention throughout Islam on a United States versus Islam conflict.

5. THE FISH IS THE LAST TO DISCOVER THE WATER

The head of the Chinese Communist Party during its most vigorous period of communization was Mao Tse-tung. One of the icons of his chairmanship was his *Little Red Book*, widely reprinted in English. It is a very small book of quotations epitomizing his wisdom that is meant to fit in a Chinese pocket. One of his universal truths is that, "The fish is the last to discover the water." What that means is that whatever social milieu we grow up in, we tend to universalize it and think that is the way everything is or must be.

Heading the revolutionary government, it was important that Mao get the point across to the population that their views of the government, its role, and its function, reflect the situation in which they grew up, which was radically different than the new China that he was vigorously and violently propagating. The point is not in any way unique to Chinese Communism. We tend to generalize as universal whatever is most common and familiar to us.

We see in Iraq the terrible consequences of our soldiers and administrators not understanding what our anticipated liberation of the people would incur: violence, vandalism, theft, destruction, the settlement of private grievances and accounts, fear of the liberator, and seeing the self-proclaimed liberator as conqueror. The failure to appreciate linguistic difficulties and the cultural differences that U.S. officers and troops would have to cope with in order to be effective, undercuts our best intentions.

6. AMERICANS ARE SELF-RIGHTEOUS

Scholars of American culture and society are in broad, but not universal, agreement that we are a self-righteous society. That is, we tend to see ourselves as morally superior to other nations and the international actions that we take as above reproach. While frequently tested and proven incorrect, that self-righteousness does persist.

As we approached Iraq in the attempt to liberate it, we in our self-righteousness saw liberation as the best thing to do. We also assumed that our system, our rules, our economy, and our polity is the only way in which a nation as socially backward as Iraq can be brought up to desirable international standards and values. How wrong can we be?

When our attitudes and claims toward Iraq were put before the global community, i.e., the United Nations, and our proposed intervention was rejected, in our self-righteousness we went ahead almost alone, unilaterally. Until recently, that word was unfamiliar. It means doing it our way and not caring about the views, interests, or proposals of other nations.

In the international arena, the theme for the last 50 years has been to promote multilateralism, that is, many sides coming together to decide what needs to be done with regard to a situation and what needs to be done to satisfy the fullest range of global interests. Our new unilateralism undermines 50 years of U.S. support for the United Nations. It reveals that strong self-righteous attitude that too often pervades American society and the actions of our elected officials.

Self-righteousness is often linked to ideology and usually reveals failure to recognize Chairman Mao's wise observation. Self-righteousness has its price. Now many countries are teaching us a lesson by giving relatively little or no military or economic aid in the reconstruction of Iraq. We made our bed and they are eager to let us lie in it. Recall Aesop's fable.

7. LET THE PEOPLE DECIDE

Thomas Jefferson and the other Founding Fathers held to some principles that formed the basis of the Declaration of Independence and the U.S. Constitution. One of those core principles is that an informed electorate, i.e., an informed citizenry, will make the right decisions. No one believes that those right decisions will always be best. But, the fundamental Jeffersonian principle is that no system is better than or more effective in the long run than one in which the decisions are based on the will of an informed electorate.

What we see in the story of Iraq before, during, and after the invasion is that the electorate, i.e., our people, was kept in the dark, misinformed, given exaggerated information, promised that there was concurrence both internally within the government and with a well-informed ally, the United Kingdom. All of that seems to melt away in the examination of the events leading to, and in the six months following, announced victory in Iraq. These systematic violations of the Jeffersonian principle tie very closely to the next point.

8. SECRECY IS A PRINCIPLE OF BUREAUCRACY

Going back to the early nineteenth century, the great German sociologist, Max Weber, observed that one of the most enduring and strongest characteristics of bureaucracy is secrecy. Bureaucracy tends to hold back information, to avoid unnecessary revelation, and, insofar as possible, to operate behind closed doors. All of which is fully understandable, because the less people who know about what goes on inside a bureaucracy, the less trouble they will create for the well-ordered government.

That is not the American way. While we do have to have agencies that are secret because of their military, intelligence, or police functions, even they have to be ventilated ... ventilated before Congress, ventilated before the state legislators, ventilated by the White House, and ventilated in discussion with each other. It appears that too little ventilation occurred in the preparations for Iraq and too much secrecy occurred among and between agencies.

It is now unclear as to who gave what advice—with what degree of authority and concurrence—to the president with regard to many of the conditions mentioned above. Questions remain about weapons of mass destruction, the extent to which al Qaeda was operating out of Iraq, the extent to which Iraq was funding foreign, i.e., non-Iraqi terrorist activities, the degree of readiness of Iraqis to welcome liberation, and the extent to which tribalism and religious differences would stand in the way or promote the movement toward a new society.

Even at the time of this writing the White House is dragging its feet in turning over preinvasion information to Congress, illustrating how strong the passion for secrecy is throughout government.

9. ALL POLITICS IS LOCAL

The great former leader of the House of Representatives, Tip O'Neil, observed after his decades of experience in U.S. politics, both local and in Congress, that what matters most for the electorate is on the local level. International issues, global issues, issues outside one's city, town, community, region, or even state count for far less than issues that are most immediate and direct in their effects.

The failure to attend to that principle led to widespread dissatisfaction with the recruitment of Army Reserves and National Guard—local actions to deal with an international situation based upon a national decision.

A few days before this writing, there was a march on Washington, D.C., to promote our immediate withdrawal from Iraq and to protest any further budget to support military action in Iraq. One newspaper said that some 150 cities were represented. In this case, local interests were more important than national interests because every dollar for Iraq is a dollar not available to deal with local issues.

The local implications of the alleged military and terrorist threats and the consequences of our involvement domestically and especially locally have been ignored, or at least overlooked and downplayed in government planning. The now daily drumbeat announcing the deaths of U.S. soldiers and civilians in Iraq is enormously powerful on the local level and is vicariously felt everywhere.

10. YOUR PLACE IN SOME HIERARCHY DETERMINES YOUR VALUES AND GOALS

From his years of study of the values that motivate people and determine their actions, the great social psychologist, Abraham Maslow, proposed a hierarchy of attitudes and behaviors in categorizing people. All of us fall somewhere on his multilayered hierarchy. For the bulk of people who are at the lowest level of socioeconomic development, namely, the poor, the uneducated, and those who are largely left out of the larger society, there is no sense of the future. They live from day to day, work from day to day, and struggle from day to day.

As people move up in prosperity—if they are fortunate and hold fairly routine ordinary low-level jobs—their focus broadens somewhat and they begin to concentrate on the things that will keep them employed. They still have a narrow, short-term, and fearful view of their position in the world. They want to hold on as tightly as they can to what they have and are deeply fearful of possible losses.

Only after one has moved up several notches does one develop attitudes and behaviors that are characteristic of the broad middle class and the much narrower upper class in the United States.

What we see now is that the people in Iraq are, to a large extent, people who fall in the lower echelons of Maslow's hierarchy; they want certitude, they want organization, they want continuity, they want security. Having destroyed much of their personal assets and having wiped out much of the job base, we are promising them the discord of the free market, the uncertainty of democratic processes, and giving them the indeterminate presence of an uncertain army that does not understand the people, their customs, and their needs.

11. IF YOU DON'T KNOW WHERE YOU ARE GOING ANY ROAD WILL GET YOU THERE

Since most of the advertised reasons for invading Iraq no longer hold water, the questions to consider are what have we gotten into, why are we there, what must we do, and when will it end?

Obviously, we cannot suddenly remove ourselves from Iraq. That would create a situation likely to be far worse than the one which brought us in. It would create a policy void in which highly aggressive Islamic fundamentalists would move in, doing on a grander scale what had happened in Afghanistan when the Taliban cooperated with al Qaeda.

We have put ourselves in a situation in which we have no sensible paths to follow, but to rehabilitate and restore the country, to undo the damage that we have done, and to work to build an alternative to a Sunni regime of Saddam Hussein acolytes or a fundamentalist takeover.

How long will it take; how much will it cost; and what must

we bring to bear? These are new questions that apparently we were totally unprepared to consider after a successful military action against the dictator and his cowardly army. What we have gotten into has certainly complexified the point above regarding an exit strategy.

12. WHO'S TO BLAME?

Our self-righteousness makes us too ready to assign blame for anything that we don't like. Blame is stultifying, negative, and crippling, because it forces us to search out who is, in a very narrow sense, responsible, and nail that person. As blame means guilt, guilt implies punishment.

The situation is far too complex to merely search to assign blame. One has to recognize that the system of events, organizations, and interactions that misled us into Iraq, which are keeping us there in unexpected circumstances, and are leading us into goals and objectives that may be unrealistic, are not the results of the actions of a single person or even a small cluster of people.

Rather, the mess reflects that the total complex of the political system, the legislative system, and the administrative system have together failed to establish rational goals, rational actions, rational behavior, and clear unequivocal plans and their subsequent implementation. We just seem to be doing it all on the fly, albeit an extremely expensive fly, while ad-hocking the operation.

It would be ideal, as many would want, to blame all of this trouble and discord on President Bush as our leader, heap the blame on his shoulders, and expel him from office at the next election. Short, sweet, to the point punishment but destructive and inappropriate. The president is technically responsible for everything that happens on his watch, including everything done by subordinates, but the reality is that a much larger range of people and institutions that feed into and feed on the White House are collectively and diffusely responsible and at fault.

However, two characteristics of the man who is now in the White House may help clarify why some of the situations described above could come about. It has been well established by those who watched Bush as governor, wrote about him as a presidential candidate, and even write about him as our president, that he has two characteristics that drive his political actions.

One of them is that he has high regard for experts and he has many experts around him. The extent to which those experts are balanced against each other—even-handed in what they present—and even aware of some of the above principles is open to argument. But relying on expertise is an important part of the president's behavior.

Second, ever since he was governor, he has had a policy of looking at a situation that calls for action, taking action that seems appropriate, and then waiting to see what occurs. Based on what occurs as a result of the previous action, he takes a second action to improve the situation, etc.

That incrementalist approach may or may not be good or the best form of political planning in a continental economy within a global world. It may tend to reinforce the short term and the ideological rather than push us to the strategic, long-term and comprehensive way of thinking.

An example of this may be the move into Iraq as a preemptive strike. While the international lawyers are busy arguing whether a preemptive strike is good or bad, legitimate or illegitimate, legal or illegal, in various national and international regions, the clear point is that it was an action that ran counter to the global community, as reflected by the United Nations.

Now we see the consequence of that preemptive strike in our inability to recruit the ready support of other wealthy nations in dealing with the Iraq situation. It is almost as if the French, Germans, Russians, and Chinese are spanking us for our misbehavior, teaching us a lesson about what globalism really involves. Refer back to Aesop's fable.

All of this remains in a state of intrinsic uncertainty until historians have had an opportunity, five, ten, or more years from now, to get at all the classified documents, all the memoirs, all the memos, and give us something resembling the truth. However that turns out, the lesson should be clear: In the future, we and our government must pay attention to the 12 points made above.

Part Three

WHAT WENT RIGHT—AND WHY?

… democracy will succeed in Iraq, because our will is firm, our word is good, and the Iraqi people will not surrender their freedom.
—President George W. Bush,
Speech in London, November 19, 2003

In fall 2003, the president of the United States boasted that since the liberation of Iraq, positive changes had occurred faster "than similar efforts in Germany and Japan after World War II."[1]

To help underline the point, in November, the White House Web site featured a remarkable story that detailed 100 accomplishments:[2] (See Appendix One: Results in Iraq: 100 Days toward Security and Freedom)

*10 Ways the Liberation of Iraq Supports the War on Terror
*10 Signs of Better Security
*10 Signs of Better Infrastructure and Basic Services
*10 Signs of Democracy
*10 Improvements in the Lives of Iraqi Children
*10 Signs of Economic Renewal
*10 Examples of International Support for the Renewal of Iraq
*10 Signs of Cultural Rebirth
*10 Steps to Improve the Lives of Iraqi Women
*10 Voices of Liberation

In this same vein, two essays hereafter highlight some of the many achievements of the U.S.-led Coalition, all the better to help you assess the *entire* complex situation. The first essay details many welcomed and overdue improvements in both the infrastructure and the quality of life for Iraqis; gains on which much further progress will depend (see the informative essay by Goertzel). The second essay tightens the focus to only the women of Iraq, explores reasons why some (though not all) Iraqi women have made remarkable strides, and what this augurs for the future (see the insightful essay by Nagpal).

FOOTNOTES

1 President George W. Bush, "Bush's Words to Britons: 'Both Our Nations Serve the Cause of Freedom,'" *New York Times*, 20 November 2003, A-14.
2 http://www.whitehouse.gov/infocus/iraq/100days/part10.html (See Appendix One).

■ Essay Five ■

REBUILDING IRAQ: WHAT HAS GONE RIGHT?

Ted Goertzel, Ph.D.

Professor of Sociology,
Rutgers-Camden

Assessing the charges and counter-charges of critics versus supporters of the Coalition's effort in postwar Iraq and finding the truth out about a situation as chaotic, complex, and many-sided as this one requires a search for less-well-known aspects of the situation, such as claims made about positive gains. All the more valuable, accordingly, is the all-too-rare account below.—Editor

Critics of the invasion of Iraq are eager to tell us about everything that has gone wrong. The weapons of mass destruction have not been found. Guerilla fighters and terrorists continue to resist. Almost every day coalition soldiers, Iraqi allies, and innocent civilians lose their lives. The cost is in the tens of billions of dollars, money that could certainly be used at home.

News reports exaggerate this dismal scenario. Television coverage is dominated by bombings, ambushes, and mortar attacks. The slow, patient work of rebuilding a nation is much harder to dramatize on the air. But, in the long run, it may be much more important.

President George W. Bush tries to draw the world's attention to the positive side of the picture. In a speech at the British foreign ministry, on November 19, 2003, he said:

> Since the liberation of Iraq, we have seen changes that could hardly have been imagined a year ago. The new Iraqi police force protects the people instead of bullying them. More than 150 Iraqi newspapers are now in circulation, printing what they choose, not what they're ordered. Schools are open, with textbooks free of propaganda. Hospitals are functioning and are well supplied. Iraq has a new currency, the first battalion of a new army, representative local governments and a governing council with an aggressive timetable for national sovereignty.

You can find mention of these accomplishments in the more highly regarded newspapers if you read them carefully. For example, on November 3, 2003, the *New York Times* published a small story reporting that:

1) 60 percent of Baghdad's residents now receive adequate water from a public system that had fallen apart during the war.
2) There has been an overall increase in student registration in school.
3) Teachers' salaries have increased to as much as $300 a month, from a maximum of $13 a month before the occupation.
4) Grants of $12 million have been given to Iraqi universities to work with American colleges.
5) All of Iraq's 240 hospitals and over 1,200 primary health clinics are open for business, although much of the equipment is still not working.
6) Health spending has increased from $16 million under Saddam Hussein to $422 under the occupation.
7) More than $100 million has been allocated to repair Baghdad's sewer system, which is currently dumping untreated sewage into the Tigris River.

The coalition effort to rebuild Iraq has four major components, as described on the Web site of the United States Agency for International Development (http://www.usaid.gov). The first is rebuilding the essential infrastructure of the country. This means restoring key services such as electricity, water, sewers, roads and bridges, telecommunications, airports, and seaports. The second is improving health and education. The third is helping the economy to grow and create jobs. The fourth is helping the Iraqis build an efficient and democratically accountable government.

IMPROVING THE INFRASTRUCTURE
By October 2003, electric power capacity in Iraq surpassed the prewar levels, and long-term repairs and scheduled maintenance were underway. The airports were open and approximately 60 nonmilitary flights were arriving and departing each day. Irreparable sections of bridges were being torn down, and 50,000 travelers a day were using a floating bridge over the Tigris River. Iraq's seaport was reopened to both passenger and cargo traffic. Work had just begun on a new fiber-optic telephone network.

IMPROVING HEALTH CARE
Over 30 million doses of vaccine had been distributed, and an estimated 3 million out of 4.5 million Iraqi children under five had been vaccinated. Hospital delivery rooms have been rehabilitated, and food supplements have been distributed to pregnant women, nursing mothers, and malnourished children. As of November 2003, rehabilitation was underway on 46 health clinics and seven had been completed. Rehabilitation of the water and sewage systems at four Baghdad hospitals was complete and work was ongoing on the other six.

IMPROVING EDUCATION
Schools throughout Iraq reopened in October 2003, and attendance surpassed preconflict levels. More than 1,774 schools had been rehabilitated for the opening. Thousands of new desks, chairs, cabinets, and supply kits were delivered. A country-wide teacher and administrator training program was

instituted. An accelerated learning program enrolled 269 girls and 267 boys in five pilot programs.

WATER SUPPLIES

Getting water running again was naturally a top priority, and immediately after the war, the United States Agency for International Development repaired more than 1,700 critical breaks in Baghdad's water network. New water plants are being built to increase capacity, and the Sweet Water Canal is being rehabilitated to bring cleaner water to the 1.3 million residents of the city of Basra. Repairing sewers will take longer, but all of Baghdad's sewer plants should be back to capacity by October 2004.

ECONOMIC GROWTH

Getting the Iraqi economy running again requires a new, stable currency and the Central Bank began replacing old dinars on October 15, 2003. Banking systems are being modernized, and laws are being revised to encourage private sector development and foreign investment. These fundamental economic changes will take time to work. In the interim, public works programs are being used to provide jobs, while rebuilding the infrastructure, and food is being distributed to prevent hunger throughout the country.

IMPROVING GOVERNMENT

Helping Iraq develop a modern, efficient, democratic government is perhaps the most controversial of tasks. An interim structure of government has been established, but there are continuing disputes about who should be on it and how much power they should have. These controversies are part of an ongoing policy of encouraging the Iraqi people to participate in governing themselves.

Many groups are active, including women's groups, so that throughout the country more than 15 million people have been represented in the process. There are training programs on governance skills, such as budgeting and record keeping, and task forces working on difficult but necessary tasks such as excavating mass graves and identifying remains.

Whatever one thinks of the wisdom of the decision to occupy Iraq, now that the coalition forces are there, it is very important that these reconstruction efforts succeed. They are important because they will bring a better life to the Iraqi people. They are also important as an example of how an Arabic country can benefit from democracy and modern lifestyles.

The Arab Human Development Report 2002, prepared for the United Nations by an outstanding team of Arab social scientists, shows that for many years the Arab world has been falling behind the Western world and leading Asian nations in many indicators of economic and social development. The authors argue that the decline has its roots in "three deficits: freedom, women's empowerment, and knowledge." The solution is modernization, women's rights, education, and democratization. If the rehabilitation of Iraq succeeds, it will be a splendid example for other countries with similar problems.

Extremist forces in the Arab world are trying to push their countries back into a dark age when women would not dare leave their homes without a male companion; when no one would be free to practice religion, open a business, or organize a social movement without permission from those who claim an exclusive mandate from God. These forces are doing everything they can to sabotage Iraq's recovery. They cannot be allowed to succeed.

REFERENCES

President George W. Bush, Speech at Whitehall Palace, London, 19 November 2003, as recorded by Federal News Service, Inc. Published in *New York Times*, 20 November 2003.

"Rebuilding Iraq: An Assessment at Six Months," *New York Times*, 3 November 2003.

United Nations Development Program, *Arab Human Development Report 2002*, Oxford University Press. Available at <http://www.undp.org/rbas/ahdr>.

USAID: Assistance for Iraq available at <http://www.usaid.gov/iraq/accomplishments>.

■ Essay Six ■

FEAR VS. FREEDOM: WOMEN OF IRAQ

Shumi Nagpal

The women of postwar Iraq are weighing their
options as never before, and the choices they
make are likely to prove quite significant. The very
fact that these Middle Eastern females have
choices is a major victory for prodemocracy elements inside and outside the country. All who favor
lives enriched by freedom and opportunity were
pleased that, in November 2003, the Governing
Council chose a woman (an Iraqi-American activist)
as its informal ambassador to the United States.[1]
The unfolding situation here warrants very close
and continuous attention, as much of the near
future of the entire region may be foreshadowed in
the state of Iraqi women tomorrow.—Editor

Fear is a terrible master. Once it takes a tight grip, it can over-
shadow reason and stifle autonomy and progress. As of early
December 2003, the women of Iraq still seem divided. Unsure if
the ground beneath is really solid, they ponder what rights they
should be striving for: "Six months after the fall of Saddam Hussein, Iraqi women are waiting on the sidelines to see if and how
they can achieve the rights they were deprived of, under 35 years
of dictatorship. In the fluid condition in which the future of the
country is being discussed, there is a debate also among women
over what rights and roles they should demand."[2]

A few may feel embarrassment because of the unexpected

ease with which the Coalition took over Iraq. For defeat of the army of one's own nation is humiliating no matter how one views the reason or outcome. Saving face is a natural human trait, but in Middle Eastern culture, this trait is more pronounced. Saving face for one's family and community despite one's personal convictions is not unusual. This cultural aspect has caused some to resist or hesitate to embrace the positive contributions made by the Coalition.

Some, "frightened by reports of a rash of kidnappings and rapes, are staying indoors, avoiding school and donning veils, frustrating those who hoped that the collapse of Saddam Hussein's regime would usher in a new era of freedom and greater equality of women."[3] There are even some legalistic Islamic men who are calling for the women of Iraq to regress behind the veil. A global cry of rejection, especially as it might come from the Islamic community regarding these retrograde pronouncements, would seem very appropriate at present.

Although fear of rapes and kidnappings are legitimate security concerns, the fear of being pushed back into the veil and oblivion is taken seriously as well. There are many Iraqi women who are fighting to preserve awakening of the minds, spirits, and voices stifled by years of dictatorship. While some women, fearing retaliation and confrontation, do slip back behind the veil, there are many others who are holding to the lifeline provided by the Coalition.

Many, perhaps the vast majority, are relieved to be free of Saddam Hussein's regime. They appreciate the many positive things the Coalition has done to assist them reclaim their rightful position in the new Iraqi government. "Britain is to help fund an Iraqi women's higher council which would advise the incoming government on how to improve the lot of 55 percent of its population."[4] "The U.S. administrator in Iraq told a gathering of Iraqi women Tuesday that they could make a vital contribution to a free and democratic society."[5]

"In a back room of the Communist party headquarters on Abu Nawas Street in Baghdad, members of the party's Women's League are engaged in an animated discussion on what the next edition of their newly launched newspaper, *Equality*, should include. Or at least what else it should include, aside from the group's slogan, pasted on all the pages: 'No to the compulsory veil.'"[6] These women are determined to uphold the beacon of hope for the youth of today and the future of tomorrow.

Perhaps anthropologist Margaret Mead said it best: "Never doubt that a small group of thoughtful, committed citizens can change the world. Indeed, it's the only thing that ever has."[7] In these tumultuous times of change, some are filled with gratitude, others with resistance, and a few with confusion. It will take only a few determined Iraqi women to make a positive difference. If the women are ever to have a voice, it is surely the Coalition that will lend them vocal chords, with firm support, until they emerge from behind curtains and under crushing concerns, to victory and wholeness.

Iraq was once among the pioneering Middle Eastern countries in that 89 percent of its women were educated. That number has plummeted during Saddam's reign to a startling 45 percent today.[8] Thanks to the determination of the Coalition and liberated Iraqis who value education, a commitment to continue building more schools will inevitably enhance the opportunities that young women can seize in their quest for a better life and eventual leadership growth.

While Iraq saw a rapid decline in women's professional and political roles, other Middle Eastern countries, such as neighboring Oman, mirrored leadership roles Iraqi women once held. Recent elections in Oman saw two women reelected to the country's advisory council: Lujaina Mohsen Darwish, a 34-year-old businesswoman, and Rahila al-Riyami, a former director of planning for education. "Darwish won 1,127 votes compared with 603 votes in the 2000 elections. Riyami also gained over her previous results, winning 741 votes compared with 421 in the last election."[9] Indeed, a remarkable vote of confidence for these emerging Middle Eastern women.

One can only imagine the heights Iraqi women might have scaled had they not been forced behind the veil by Saddam's regime. Although the Coalition has loosened the chains that kept

Iraqi women dormant, sexist and stifling legalism proposed by some Islamic men is threatening to tighten the chains again. These legalistic men will not go away just because the Coalition is temporarily in Iraq. If women want to emerge and once again play key roles in their government, and stand shoulder to shoulder with some of their counterparts in the Middle East, they must break the chains of repression imposed by these men. They must embrace the rope of freedom extended by the Coalition, even if some are left with "rope burns."

Renovation and rejuvenation of mind, body, and spirit sometimes comes at a steep price, but the results are usually worth the effort. If these women allow their traditional oppressors elbowroom, serious setbacks will loom in their futures. In a critical time of uncertainties, the women of Iraq—divided as they are by ethnicity, social class, and degree of modernity—must seize opportunities, voice their desires, and stand together. If they remain divided, they will fall; united, they will surely stand.

FOOTNOTES

1 Susan Sachs, "Iraq Picks American as Ambassador to U.S.," *New York Times*, 23 November 2003, 16.
2 Peyman Pejman, "Iraq: Women's Rights Put on Hold," Common Dreams News Center, 4 October 2003. Available at <http://www.commondreams.org/headlines03/1004-06.htm>.
3 Susan Milligan, "Iraqi Women Recoiling in Fear of Crime," *Boston Globe*, 4 August 2003.
4 Katarina Kratovac, "U.S. Administrator: Iraqi Women to Play Key Role in Democracy Building," Associated Press, 7 October 2003.
5 Sarah Hall, "U.K. to Fund Women's Council in Iraq," *The Guardian*, 17 October 2003.
6 Kim Ghattas, "Iraqi Women Fight to Redeem the Promise of Freedom," *Financial Times*, 3 September 2003.
7 Margaret Mead (1901–1978)—U.S. Anthropologist.
8 Tina Susman, "Women of Iraq Fear the Future," *Newsday*, 16 June 2003.
9 *Gulf Today*, 6 October 2003.

Part Four

WHAT MIGHT WE DO NEXT?

*We will help the Iraqi people establish a peaceful and democratic
country in the heart of the Middle East, and by doing so, we
will defend our people from danger.*
—President George W. Bush,
Speech in London, November 19, 2003

In this, the largest section of the book, we tackle the bottom-
line question: How might we achieve the soundest of our goals
during the postwar occupation of Iraq? Progress here will be
very difficult, for we are "chilled by the metastasizing al Qaeda,
the resurgent Taliban, and Baathist thugs armed with deadly
booby traps; the countless, nameless terror groups emerging in
Turkey, Morocco, Indonesia, and elsewhere; the vicious attacks
on Americans, Brits, aid workers and their supporters in Iraq,
Afghanistan, and Turkey."[1]

As the best defense against fear and fear-mongering is a creative life-enriching offense, seven essays hereafter explore pragmatic programs of reform, each worth your careful
consideration.

The first boldly prescribes strong antidotes to the threat
posed everywhere, from Baghdad to Lower Manhattan, by suicide bombers (see the stark essay by Radu). The second makes
a novel case for the liberating employ of religion and religious
freedom, always a contentious and consequential factor in
Middle East matters (see the creative essay by Seiple). The
third sensitively reviews what young people can learn from
their folks—and vice versa—where "hot button" matters like
the Second Gulf War are concerned (see the engaging essay by
Shaw). The fourth calls on all of us to value and employ our

precious right to vote, and thereby influence foreign affairs (see the empowering essay by Furin).

Taking still another tact, the fifth essay confronts the far-reaching question: "If you opposed the War before its start, where might you be now? Why? And, so what?" (See the provocative essay by Wright) The sixth essay explains why we MUST soon reduce our reliance on Middle East oil (see the learned essay by Liebman). Finally, the closing essay asks us to imagine the situation in Iraq today if the U.S.-led Coalition had not forced a change in regime. Imagine what might happen if we withdraw with much left unachieved, including the restoration of law and order, creation of an independent judiciary, implementation of an Iraqi form of democracy, assurances of new rights for women, provision of new educational opportunities for the young, protection of new civil rights, new grounds for hope, and concrete evidence of reform and progress.

Imagine. And the writer below does just that. Jennings' essay is thereby a fitting close to a volume sent to press at a time of extraordinary uncertainty, a time when reminding ourselves of the best of the White House vision here would seem more vital than ever.

FOOTNOTE

1 Maureen Dowd, "Scaring Up Votes," *New York Times*, 23 November 2003, WK-11

RADICAL ISLAM
AND SUICIDE BOMBERS

Michael Radu, Ph.D.

Cochairman of the Center on Terrorism,
Counter Terrorism, and Homeland Security,
Foreign Policy Research Institute,
Philadelphia, Pa.

Who become suicide bombers? Why? What motivates them? What part does religion play in their motivation? Have any countries had any success in limiting the toll these killers take? What could the United States do to help the world meet this growing threat, one we know all too (bloody) well from 9/11 and fear we will "meet" again?—Editor

---

To most Westerners, especially Americans, the almost regular and predictable murder of Israeli civilians of all ages seems both incomprehensible and, precisely because of its regularity and frequency, unsurprising.

The phenomenon, however, has stirred some interest in a media previously immune to serious analysis of terrorism in general and within American academia, which was traditionally uninterested in terrorism.

Since the early 1980s, when the Lebanese Shia Hezbollah (with Iranian Khomeinist funds and training) and the Sri Lankan Liberation Tigers of Tamil Eelam—LTTE (Marxists/Hindus/Tamil secessionists) initiated the routine use of suicide terrorists as an instrument of war, suicide bombers have been active in Sri Lanka, Turkey, India, Lebanon, Israel, Russia, the United States, and Indonesia.

Failed suicide bombing attempts—including the use of air-craft—are known from France, Spain, and Turkey, and successful attempts have been made elsewhere by citizens or residents of Germany and the United Kingdom.

With the exception of the LTTE's acts, all these terrorist acts were committed by Muslims, and of those, all except those by the PKK/Kadek in Turkey and Yasser Arafat's Al Aqsa Martyrs Brigades were committed by members of openly Islamist groups.

These groups operate more like religious sects under the absolute control of a charismatic leader. The leaders are God-like figures of absolute political and spiritual authority.

And then there is suicide bombers' targeting, again a religiously related variable. The LTTE targeted politicians—they murdered a former Indian prime minister and a Sri Lankan president—but not civilians, unless as "collateral damage." The PKK suicide bombers also targeted Turkish military police or jandarma, not civilians. By contrast, the Islamist terrorists have targeted civilians since the start: Jews if possible, Americans, Australians, Indians, or other Western "crusaders" and assorted "nonbelievers."

The suicide bomber terrorist phenomenon is a growing element in the international terrorists' arsenal, but it remains a weapon with a religious background. It was, and is everywhere, a weapon of the relatively educated: Tamil Hindu women mixed well at Buddhist electoral meetings in Sri Lanka; Palestinian high school and university students posed as Israelis; and Western-educated Islamists trained to murder thousands in the United States on 9/11, hundreds in Bali, and many in Casablanca and Riyadh.

Exactly who are these suicide bombers, widely described as "martyrs" in Muslim, not just Islamist, opinion? They are certainly not "martyrs" in the Christian sense—people who were killed for their faith—but murderers, people who killed themselves in order to murder others.

Most choose innocent and defenseless victims simply for the psychological value their actions will bring about—the "theater" aspect of terrorism. Most are relatively privileged, educated young people, and a growing number are women. A few, such as Chechnya's "blackwidows," have deeply personal reasons for their actions, primarily revenge for the loss of family members; others are simply lost souls who have lost all moral standards; but most are fanatics—products of well-planned recruitment and indoctrination schemes.

What they all share is Roman philosopher Seneca's opinion that he who does not prize his own life threatens that of others. And suicide terrorism works: According to Israeli sources, during the past three years suicide bombers were responsible for 50 percent of Israeli fatalities, while making only 0.5 percent of the total number of terrorist attacks.

Is there a "solution" to the suicide-bomber phenomenon? If "solution" means putting a stop to it in absolute terms the answer has to be no—precisely because Seneca was right.

Could the incidence of such actions be limited and drastically reduced? Yes, and it has been done, in Algeria, Turkey, and Israel. At the same time, we must provide support and understanding for, rather than persistent criticism of, those Muslim regimes, whether in Cairo, Islamabad, Rabat, or Algiers, undemocratic as they may be for the human rights fundamentalists of the UN and nongovernmental organizations. Not just because perfection is often the enemy of good, but also because, being the first in the line of fire from terrorists, they have the motivation and the record of success against them.

Ultimately, the suicide bomber is just another tool in the arsenal of the international terrorist group. For the bomber, religion is the basic motivation. Their mission is legitimized by a supreme charismatic leader or Islamic cleric; special recruiters bring the suicide candidate together with the group. Eliminating the enablers—the recruiters and ideologists—wherever they are (mostly in London, Pakistan, and Saudi Arabia) must therefore be the first step in eliminating the problem.

■ Essay Eight ■

RELIGION AND THE NEW GLOBAL COUNTERINSURGENCY

Chris Seiple[1]

President of the Institute for Global Engagement,
Philadelphia, Pa.

The essay below contends that progress
hinges on our soon gaining "a better understanding of such words as terrorism, insurgency,
strategy, and, our greatest weapon, religious
freedom. We must be willing to mobilize and
employ all the elements of power to wage
it.... And we must be prepared to make a generational commitment to see it through." —Editor

---

*The first, the supreme, the most far-reaching act of judgment that
the statesman and commander have to make is to establish the kind of
war on which they are embarking; neither mistaking it for, nor trying
to turn it into, something that is alien to its nature. This is the first
of all strategic questions and the most comprehensive.*[2]
—Karl von Clausewitz

As the summer of 2003 came to an end, Americans were
caught up in a false debate about the number of troops
needed to "win the peace" in Iraq. The amount of time spent
on this oxymoron reveals how much we Americans still don't

understand about the nature of security in the twenty-first century.

Now is the time to revisit the words and phrases we use to describe the portentous global struggle we are now engaged in, ensuring that those words have some relation to its nature. This is foremost the responsibility of both the statesman and commander. Although President Bush is right to call it a "different kind of war," we are well on our way to making it "alien to its nature."

The words we use to describe the war tell us how we think about its nature and implicitly describe how we intend to fight it. Unfortunately, the words we are now using to describe the war to both the American people and the world audience obfuscate the issue as much as they illuminate.

Today the United States is said to be fighting a "global war on terrorism," building an "empire," and defeating "dead-enders" with a "new American way of war." Too often these words cloud our analysis and prevent us from properly understanding the nature of this war and how to wage it. In fact, if we are to win this war, we must have a better understanding of such words as terrorism, insurgency, strategy, and, our greatest weapon, religious freedom. We must be willing to mobilize and employ all the elements of power to wage it. We must be able to effectively communicate the nature and stakes of the struggle. And we must be prepared to make a generational commitment to see it through.

THE "GLOBAL WAR ON TERRORISM"

This phrase is perhaps the most unfortunate to emerge since 9/11. Terrorism is the "calculated use of unlawful violence or threat of unlawful violence to inculcate fear."[3] It is intended to coerce or to intimidate governments or societies in the pursuit of goals that are generally political, religious, or ideological. Eradicating terrorism is a noble goal, but declaring war on terrorism is nonsensical. Terrorism is a means not an end; a symptom not an enemy.

If we do not wage a specific war against a specific enemy—

all the while explaining and explaining again who our enemy is, what their goals are, and why we should work to frustrate those goals—our words will be hijacked for the purposes of others. Already both sides in the Middle East have used President Bush's "global war on terrorism" language to explain their own questionable actions. The Russians have done the same in Chechnya.

Nor are these rhetorical escalations a new phenomenon. Who can forget the soaring oratory of President Kennedy's inaugural address, compelling us to "bear any burden, pay any price"? Who can deny that this vision provided the foundation for getting involved in Vietnam through assassination or supporting any other dictator who happened not to be a Communist?

We must be very specific about who we are fighting and why. Certainly we are at war, but we are not at war with terrorism. This is a global war, and victory requires more than conventional armies and mentalities.

We are in fact engaged in a three-front global counterinsurgency against very specific people and organizations. The first front is the attack on the terrorists themselves and their infrastructure. The second front is the attack on the conditions that make terrorism a viable weapon for our adversaries. The third front is the public diplomacy that explains the first two in a way that builds American credibility and legitimacy, in part, through making this war everyone's and not just America's.

THE "NEW AMERICAN WAY OF WAR"
The quick U.S. victories in Afghanistan and Iraq have been much ballyhooed in the press as the new American way of war, even called the "Rumsfeld Doctrine." There is nothing new about it. The notion of striking quickly and deeply with flanks unprotected, using speed as security, is as old as war itself. Genghis Khan would certainly recognize this form of warfare. So, too, would the father of the Blitzkrieg, Heinz Guderian, as would his one-time division commander, Erwin Rommel, who once told his Afrika Korps to simply "attack, attack, attack."

This kind of "maneuver warfare," while generally anomalous to the U.S. military preference for battles of attrition and annihilation, is by no means foreign to U.S. military leaders, having been practiced by Stonewall Jackson in the Shenandoah Valley, General Patton's 3rd Army in Europe, and the Marine landing at Inchon in Korea. And since the end of the Vietnam War, all services have, to a greater or lesser extent, emphasized maneuver. Make no mistake, the military victories in Afghanistan and Iraq are of the same fabric and equally brilliant. But they are not new.

What these two victories do signal, however, is the arrival of a new expeditionary age. The distance over which U.S. forces can now conduct these maneuvers, and the speed and precision with which they can perform them, is unprecedented. What was once the comparative advantage of the United States Marine Corps is now the modus operandi of all the services— indeed, the Department of Defense as a whole (and soon, if we are to win, the entire national security establishment).

Witness the redesign of U.S. bases overseas from huge depots and creature comforts to skeletal springboards for quick response and/or preemptive action. These bases are conceptually reminiscent of U.S. Naval officer Alfred Thayer Mahan's desire for coaling stations around the world. They smack of both necessity and empire.

The victories in Afghanistan and Iraq, impressive as they were, involved the application of conventional military forces against an enemy who could largely be identified in the course of battle. However, after each of the "conventional" victories— after the adversary had quit the battlefield, melted away, and begun to confront our forces with different tactics—U.S. forces found it far more difficult to bring operations to strategic closure. It turned out that operations in these conflicts were merely battlefield victories, not strategic ones.

The "new" American way of war, then, focused on destruction of conventional armies, may already be obsolete. To keep from making the same mistake that we committed in Vietnam, we must accept that the United States, for the first time, is fighting a *global* counterinsurgency in which conventional military capabilities must be subordinate to, and supportive of, the synergistic combination of all the elements of power in support of our wartime policy. This is the new American way of war.

INSURGENCY

An insurgency features a military force that is not capable of fighting on the conventional battlefield. It uses hit-and-run tactics, counting on a sympathetic people to support it. Chairman Mao Tse-tung once said that "As the fish are among the sea, so too is the guerrilla among the people." Because the people are the center of gravity in this kind of war, it is foremost a psychological one, waged in the proverbial "hearts and minds" through socio-economic-political means.

In general, the guerrilla must therefore possess a consistent ideology that not only explains why he is fighting but also provides tangible benefit to the people of the world to come once the guerrilla is victorious (with the latter being more important in the beginning). For example, the Palestinian people support Hamas not so much for their terrorism or their ideology but because of their social and health programs. It is a time-tested way of creating your own sea to swim in.

And it takes time. Mao, who led the most successful insurgency in the history of the world, spent the early years making his political ideas relevant to the peasants. He also taught his guerrillas to treat the people right. For example, if a guerrilla was visiting a peasant home, it was a rule to always put the door back covering the entrance. Hearts and minds are not won overnight. They are won one life at a time by a sustained and consistent message backed by the same action.

The global insurgency that we face has two distinct levels, the strategic and the operational, with two kinds of insurgents, the international and the local. Strategically, the United States is fighting an international insurgent wherever he reveals himself in the world. These insurgents are of the al Qaeda kind—well-funded, linked in their hatred of the United States, and motivated by a truncated religion that Muslims of true faith disavow.

Operationally, the United States is fighting the international insurgent in particular countries where they sometimes work with local or national insurgents (Iraq, Afghanistan, Philippines). The local insurgent (the Taliban or former Baathists) may not share the motivation of the internationals, but they have a common enemy in the United States, and, increasingly, they share a common tactic—terrorism—making it hard to distinguish between them. They sometimes also have the veneer of sharing a religion. In the hands of the right political entrepreneur, religion can both unite these two types of insurgents and recruit and retain more of them.

No place better illustrates this confluence of local and international insurgents and the use of terrorism than Iraq, where the internationals are descending. There are many good things going on in the majority of Iraq. But the Sunni (central) portion of the country is in the midst of full-scale insurgency fought by local and international Sunnis. It will be a key tactical theater in the broader global counterinsurgency. If we are successful there, our broader strategic aims will be materially advanced.

One point, however. Some people insist on referring to the enemy in Iraq as "dead-enders." This phrase is denigrating to our troops who fight and who are killed by them. William Manchester wrote in *Goodbye Darkness* (an autobiography of his time in the Pacific as a Marine) that calling the Japanese troops "fanatics" belittled the bravery necessary to defeat them. I agree. Our adversaries are committed, at times both brave and "fanatical," insurgents. If we don't show respect for the goals and tactics of these insurgents, we will not be able to defeat them.

COUNTERINSURGENCY

If you want to catch the fish in the sea, then you'd better learn to think like a fish. Similarly, if you want to suppress an insurgency, then you've got to think like the insurgent, or guerrilla. Fighting guerrillas is not something Americans are naturally good at. The examples we have—General George Crook along the Mexican border, the *Small Wars Manual* of the Marines' experience in the Caribbean and Central America during the 1920s and 1930s, David Hackworth's battalion in Vietnam—are too few and forgotten. The actual fighting against the insurgents will require new levels of excellence in intelligence-gathering and the adaptation of forgotten tactics to the nature of new operational environments.

At the end of the day, however, fighting these insurgents, as well as winning the war, is predicated on the sea in which they swim—the people. It is the people who will provide the necessary intelligence to find and defeat the insurgents. It is the people who will work with us once it is clearly and repeatedly communicated to them what our purpose is in that particular theater of operations. And it is the people—once educated by their own Sunni and Shiite leaders—who will find the manipulation of their faith by insurgents abhorrent.

There must be a coherent and cohesive application of power, of which military power is, ultimately, but one minor component. It requires not only the synergistic use of all the elements of national (and yes, international) power but a comprehensive understanding of the religious environment in which that power will be applied, and a profound sense of strategy and the responsibilities of leadership.

STRATEGY & GRAND STRATEGY

Unfortunately, one does not come across these terms, in a meaningful manner, that often. Without a constant regard for them, however, the war upon which we have embarked can become the ends instead of the means. John Lewis Gaddes, the preeminent Cold War historian, defines strategy as "The process by which ends are related to means, intentions to capabilities, objectives to resources."[4] Such a definition allows priorities to become clear. By definition, strategy is interactive and fluid; it is always changing to best reflect the nature of the environment and thus influence it.

Grand strategy, as Paul Kennedy notes, is "the capacity of the nation's leaders to bring together all of the elements [of power], both military and nonmilitary, for the preservation and enhancement of the nation's long-term (that is, in wartime and peacetime) best interests."[5] Grand strategy requires well-defined policy goals, interim objectives, and measures of effectiveness for each of the elements of power applied. It requires that we wage peace with the same gravitas that we make war.

LEADERSHIP

Global polls suggest that most people around the world like Americans but take exception to the policies of their government. Always true somewhere about some government, the polls do show that there is misunderstanding of the stakes involved and the kind of leadership that the United States offers. It also begs a good definition of leadership.

Leadership has been defined many ways. One value-neutral definition is, put simply, the process of getting the job done with what you've got. To my mind, however, leadership is more than this neutral observation. Leadership is the external manifestation of internal values. If one exhibits values, one attracts others who want to experience and/or learn about those values. In short, leaders lead because of who they are. The same is true of nations.

What is America? For me, America is equal opportunity for the pursuit of happiness. This opportunity is built on responsible freedom, a freedom that demonstrates tolerance for difference amidst the pursuit of happiness. As George Washington wrote to Moses Seixas and the Newport Synagogue regarding religious freedom in August of 1790: "All possess alike liberty of conscience ... For happily the Government of the United States, which gives to bigotry no sanction, to persecution no assistance, requires only that they who live under its protection should demean themselves as good citizens, in giving it on all occasions their effectual support."[6]

In essence, to be American is to demonstrate tolerance/respect toward the many allegiances the peoples and groups of this land possess within the greater allegiance of one people to one constitution. We pledge allegiance to the nation because it is the keeper of this idea.

It is thus a double-paradox that we must account for as we lead and wage a global counterinsurgency at home and abroad. First, our greatest "weapon" is the concept of responsible freedom and religious tolerance. This weapon, once implemented as a mature civil society, inherently leaves us vulnerable as a society to those who would destroy our ideas. This is the price of freedom, the penalty of leadership.

To wield our greatest weapon in this global counterinsurgency, there must be truth-in-advertising as we account for the reality that many in the world today fear the United States more than bin Laden or North Korea. Ridiculous to most Americans, we cannot dismiss this perception in a war for hearts and minds. Perception is reality. To change this reality—that is, to wage war on the third front of public diplomacy—the United States must act as the leader that it is, as a "hegemon," not an empire. Not only is this consistent with its founding values, it is the most practical for waging a global counterinsurgency.

EMPIRE AND HEGEMONY

The difference between Republicans and Democrats, the old joke goes, is that the Democrats apologize for the empire. As I watched our special forces come and go from my Tashkent hotel in the aftermath of 9/11, it was hard to deny that American power reaches the most remote places, i.e., that the United States is an empire. "Empire," however, is a two-dimensional word from a by-gone era characterized by the hard ground and hard power of geography and military might. While these characteristics remain the foundation of global stability, they alone do not accurately embody the American idea and thus our leadership.

In an empire, mirror images and military solutions dominate foreign policy. In the Vietnam War movie *Full Metal Jacket*, for example, the battalion commander tells the private: "Don't ya know son, inside every Vietnamese national is an American trying to get out. Now jump on board for the big win." In an empire, bigger military hammers are needed everywhere as every nuance of policy takes on the form of a nail. Hegemony is different because it leads from within, applying a true grand strategy in which the military is not the piggyback, or piggybank, for every other element of national power.

We are living in an era of accidental American hegemony.

Hegemony has come to mean a regional or great power's influence over other states. But its Greek root, *hegemon*, simply means "leader." Hegemony is leadership. American hegemony is accidental because it was not sought. But like it or not, the United States is the 800-pound gorilla on the world stage, and its action or inaction will influence every major issue in the world.

Responsible leadership, however, begins with the organization we use to implement our national power here and overseas. For any organization to be effective, it must be organic. An effective organization is not "alien to" the nature of the environment in which it is applied. Our problem today is that we think the way we're organized—and we are still organized to win the Cold War.

Peace is still uncertain in Afghanistan and Iraq because we did not think through, or fund, the other elements of national power to do their job. As a result, the military gets left holding the bag despite the fact that it is not educated or trained for such missions. And while such missions are normal amidst the transition from war to peace, their continuation by military means helps no one. Beyond literally hurting the military, it is at this point that we begin to lose the initiative with the very people we are trying to help.

If we are to get our military back to its comparative advantage of breaking things, then we have to operationalize the relevant elements of power in order to build things, namely states. For that to take place, we need a new kind of interagency specialist, one who (a) thinks holistically across the elements of power, (b) takes into account the interrelated dimensions of theaters of operations (e.g., the socio-economic-political dimensions of Iraq and how they inform our actions as well as our public diplomacy), and (c) understands the bedrock role of religion—both positively and negatively—in today's global challenges.

There is but one way to create such a specialist: through "joint" education. Only education changes behavior. We absolutely need the Goldwater-Nichols equivalent for those involved in the interagency. (The 1986 Goldwater-Nichols Act requires that military personnel who want to be promoted to the highest ranks be educated together). The result is a common culture based on common words and common understandings. As Lord George Robertson, the NATO Secretary General, told reporters in Kabul this past July, NATO is effective because of its "habit of training and educating together."[7]

In sum, Hegemonists are holistic, educated to comprehend and work effectively in cultures that seek freedom in their own way. Hegemonists understand that rule-of-law is transcendent while democracy, perhaps, is not. Hegemonists recognize that this global insurgency is religious and that it will require a better understanding of religious freedom if we are to be secure.

RELIGIOUS FREEDOM: THE MISSING DIMENSION OF SECURITY

The missing ingredient to our global counterinsurgency's grand strategy—ironically enough for this hegemon of persecuted origins—is religious freedom. Thomas Jefferson called religious freedom the "first freedom," for where there was religious freedom so, too, was there the right to gather, associate, and have freedom of the press.

Two critical issues, however, prevent us from incorporating this *primus inter pares* value into an operational grand strategy. First, while tolerance is what we seek, terror is the other side of the religious freedom coin. It was too much religious freedom in Northwest Pakistan that allowed the madrassas to teach rote hate. It was an American-constructed constitution in Japan that protected the religious sect Aum Shinriyko from investigation as it grew into a billion-dollar entity that eventually used saran gas in the Tokyo subways. The potential for a truncated religion to be legally protected as it sows actionable hate is in the seed of every form of tolerance that we plant.

Second, in our own society, we fear introducing religion into any discussion, especially in interagency circles, because it might impugn the separation of church and state, a wailing wall that too many worship. In Iraq, for example, Sheik al-Sadr— the son of Mohammed Sadiq al-Sadr, the Iraqi Shiite Ayatollah assassinated by Hussein in 1999 for having a network that transcended tribal and religious divides—wanted to establish an Institute for Religious Tolerance with Sunni colleagues in order to address the root causes of the violence. It was next to impossible for our government to support because it includes the word "religion." We have reached the tragic-ironic point where we cannot pursue national security interests related to religious freedom because it might threaten the Constitution.

We have separated church and state in the name of good governance with good result. But the casualty has been analysis, and we will soon suffer additional casualties if we do not address religion and religious freedom as a realpolitik factor. U.S. national policy must find a way to incorporate these factors into our grand strategy. By encouraging a culturally congruent form of religious freedom in Afghanistan and Iraq, we ask the people to celebrate the best of their faith. As we do so, we take away the recruiting pool of the insurgents because people better versed in their faith will not fall for perversions of it. As they learn more about their faith, they will recognize it as a faith that calls for the tolerance of others.

It will take time. And it will take nuance as we partner with the right Muslim leaders without co-opting them by sheer association. But not to take this kind of action is to ignore the realpolitik reality of this global insurgency, while forgetting who we are and where we came from. Besides, a mature understanding of religious freedom is the greatest preemptive weapon against religious terrorism that we, and the world, possess.

CONCLUSION

The words we use are important. Our current clichés do not reveal the nature of the security environment we live in and, in fact, camouflage it with Cold War concepts that invite failure. We are waging a different kind of war. That war is a global counterinsurgency, and it requires a grand strategy that incorporates all the elements of national power as well as a much better understanding of religion.

Wielding this national power adroitly will require a reorganization of our national security establishment and the creation of new interagency leaders. It will not be easy and it will take time. But we can and will win because the key to winning this war—religious freedom—is already a part of us. We just have to remember.

FOOTNOTES

1 This article originally appeared on 1 September 2003 on the IGE Web site. The author wishes to thank Robert O. Work for his helpful comments on an earlier version of this article.

2 Karl Von Clausewitz, *On War*, eds. and trans. Michael Howard and Peter Paret, Princeton, N.J.: Princeton University Press, 1976, 88-89.

3 *Department of Defense Dictionary of Military and Associated Terms*, Joint Publication 1-02, 12 April 2001 (As amended through June 5, 2003), 531. Available at <http://www.dtic.mil/doctrine/jel/new_pubs/jp1_02.pdf>.

4 John Lewis Gaddes, *Strategies of Containment* (New York: Oxford University Press, 1982), viii.

5 Paul Kennedy, *Grand Strategy in War and Peace* (New Haven, Conn.: Yale University Press, 1991), 5.

6 Letter to Moses Seixas from President George Washington, retrieved from the web in July 2001. Available at <http://www.loc.gove/exhibits/treasures/trm006.html>.

7 As quoted in "What Does NATO Deployment Mean for the Alliance?" by Breffni O'Rourke, *Radio Free Europe Magazine*, retrieved 13 August 2003. Available at <http://www.rferl.org/nca/features/2003/08/12082003201928.asp>.

LIVING HISTORY, MAKING HISTORY, AND LISTENING TO STORIES

Peter Shaw

High school history teacher and
Activist with Jobs with Justice and
Portland Central America Solidarity Committee

Unless and until we get better at talking with and especially at listening to one another, we will accomplish less, and enjoy life less than any of us want. This is especially true where families are concerned. The so-called Generation Gap isn't funny, or infrequent, or slight in the toll it takes. All the more valuable, therefore, is the unique account below of how one son and his father have achieved a better-than-average way of relating. They actually trade ideas with one another about the Iraq War and its continuing challenge, and thereby model a sound "way to go" for all of us.—Editor

---

When I was a boy of 14, my father was so ignorant I could hardly stand to have the old man around. But when I got to be 21, I was astonished at how much the old man had learned in seven years.
—Mark Twain

My father and I don't see eye to eye on many issues, and I suspect on many occasions he reflects upon the possibility that the nurse in the hospital switched me with another baby and put me in the bassinet marked "Shaw"; a cruel joke inflicted upon him by a cruel world. The horror, the horror! Our invasion of Iraq was another event upon which we disagreed.

On April 5, 2003, we talked about the war which had been going on for 17 days, and I was more ratcheted up than usual. I had just come back from an antiwar march, and thoughts of slaughtered people in Iraq and lying administrations in Washington, D.C., hell-bent on further expansion and its accompanying violence were swirling in my mind. Our debate was more lively than usual, or at least I was more lively than usual. I found it so obvious that what we were doing was wrong.

Was Saddam Hussein a bad man? If you are in the running for understatement of the year, yes. Brutal, vicious, and horrible are more appropriate words. The images of his gassing Kurds and Iranians, as well as stories of his iron-fisted tactics of brutally repressing any and all opposition, were all over the news.

Should we have supported regime change in Iraq? I think so, but I also believe there are other ways of doing this. History holds examples of people rising up against their oppressive rulers. The people of Iran rose up against and overthrew the Shah; the people of Romania bid farewell to the tyrant Ceauşescu; the Filipino people kicked dictator Ferdinand Marcos out of power (the Shah, Ceauşescu, and Marcos were all supported by the United States); and the people of the Soviet Union finally threw away the shackles of that brutal system. Certainly an external power bombing civilian populations is not the only way to affect change, although, as shown in the invasion of Iraq, it proves extremely effective against a country which cannot defend itself. It also puts a foreign power in charge of the country instead of the country's own people.

For me, dropping bombs on innocent people was unacceptable, and the people who were talking about all the awful slaughters Saddam had committed not only neglected to mention how we had consistently supported him right up to his invasion of Kuwait in 1990 but also never mentioned the murderous sanctions we imposed upon Iraq after the first Gulf War that resulted in the deaths of between $1/2$–$1\,1/2$ million people,[1] while seemingly strengthening Saddam's grip on power.[2]

My father, on the other hand, thought we needed to attack. It was as obvious to him as my feelings were to me. Here was a maniacal tyrant who, regardless of possession of weapons of mass destruction, posed a threat to the United States.

Was Saddam involved in the bombings of September 11, 2001? No, my dad did not buy that. He is a logical man, and there was no proof. Likewise he knew, despite polls that showed many Americans believed otherwise, there was no link between Saddam and al Qaeda: quite logical considering they hate each other. Osama bin Laden had even called for the Iraqis to remove Saddam from power.[3]

Could Saddam work with other terrorists and help commit acts of terrorism in the future? Yes, thought my father, and we could not afford to assume otherwise. What about all the Iraqis—victims of Saddam's regime—who would die under the U.S. assault? My dad thought we had to get rid of Saddam, and he knew many would die doing so.

My father was born in 1925, grew up in New York City during the Great Depression, and as soon as he was of age, served in the 8th Army Air Force during World War II. Adolph Hitler was waging wars of aggression, and he was also slaughtering Jews, Gypsies, homosexuals, and Jehovah's Witnesses. If there was ever evil incarnate, he was it, and he wanted to spread his Aryan dream throughout the world.

My father was the tail gunner in a bomber that ran missions over Germany. Thanks to people like my father who understood such dreams were nightmares, the Nazis were defeated. While I would eschew describing him with terms like "the greatest generation," I could rattle off a lengthy list of superlatives.

How many people did my father's plane's bombs kill? I never asked, and he probably does not know. That is part of the nature of modern war. It is impersonal. There are no bodies; only numbers. But he knows those bombs killed people. I would imagine that even with the pride he took in helping vanquish Hitler, he also feels something I hope I never have the misfortune of feeling: the pain and suffering the German people experienced as a result of those bombs he helped deliver. Not all Germans were Nazis, and my dad is, after all, human.

So my dad knows war, and my dad knows death. He was an instrument in delivering it and the world is a better place because of what he did.

Like my father, I was raised Catholic, and while I have abandoned the religion, there are elements of the faith that I hope still guide my life. One of these is the importance of ethics—certainly a nebulous and unwieldy term but, nonetheless, fathomable enough to us as individuals. The American invasion of Iraq was, for me, a violation of principles I try to uphold, not to mention those of the charter of the United Nations. We would kill thousands of people, and though we would be getting rid of Saddam Hussein, history has shown that when a power engages in such ventures now tabbed "humanitarian interventions" the results rarely create freedom for those who we are freeing from shackles.[4]

My father felt the war with Iraq was not a matter of ethics. It was one of practicality, and practicality dictated that we remove Saddam Hussein from power. This had nothing to do with removing him because of his horrible crimes. My father knew the most heinous of those crimes had been performed with—at the least—our tacit approval. He knew current Secretary of Defense Donald Rumsfeld had shook hands with Saddam in 1983, while serving as an emissary for President Ronald Reagan.[5] And he knew that President George H.W. Bush might have been able to remove Saddam from power by supporting a peoples' revolution but, instead, provided no support, allowing Saddam to crush the revolt.

What he also knew during the days leading up to March 19, 2003, was that Saddam posed a threat to his existence, my existence, my brother's existence, my mom's existence, and millions of others' existences. Practicality (and love, if in a limited sense) dictated we get rid of him now, and if thousands of Iraqis died along the way, that was grim reality.

For me, choosing practicality is an ethical choice. In the case of the invasion of Iraq, such practicality was not some abstraction but a horror that would be visited upon the Iraqi people. I found it bizarre that this man who had helped raise me in a religion that purportedly followed the teachings of Jesus was telling me the slaughter of Iraqis did not matter; that to prevent possible terrorism we had an obligation to resort to real terrorism. There was certainly a moral dilemma that was made abundantly clear by both a sign at the rally that day that stated, "Who Would Jesus Bomb?" and in the writings of Howard Zinn, who noted there is no flag big enough to cover the shame of killing innocent people.

A fundamental moral principle of ethics is that if you declare an action good for others, then it is good for you. Likewise, if you declare an action not good for you, then it is not good for others. Among many who have understood this principle was Jesus who condemned as hypocrites those who lived by a different set of standards than those they applied to others.

Keeping this elementary moral principle in mind, I asked my father if he felt that other countries had the right to bomb the United States because we had nuclear weapons. This was, of course, lunacy, but the question was one of ethics, not practicality. I assume the same would hold true for demanding that United Nations weapons inspectors have access to every nook and cranny of any U.S. corporation creating or working with chemicals. Thus, bombing Iraq to get rid of some potential nuclear weapons owned by a tyrant was practical but getting rid of the same weapons owned in far greater numbers by the only country ever to use one was not.

My dad also noted that there was a United Nations resolution that authorized the use of force against Iraq if it was found in violation of any rules set down by the United Nations. However, despite the Bush administration's claims, the resolution did not grant the United States the right to determine whether Iraq was in "material breach" of its obligations regarding inspections. Furthermore, the resolution did not authorize the United States to decide what would be done in the case of a breach by Iraq. Such decisions were to be made by the full Security Council.

I get pretty fired up about things for which I have a passion, so my dad's and my conversation got pretty heated but, then again, so do many things in our conversations. I also got heated when some friends of mine said my father was stupid after I described my exchanges with him. My father—and yes, I am quite biased about this—is many things but stupid is not one of them. He is loving, caring, generous, trustworthy, trusting, and a whole host of other qualities of which I may partially attain one or two on my best days. He is also intelligent.

My point here is not to defend my father. He needs no defense. My father and I continued to discuss the war, not despite our disagreements but because of them.

We can learn a great deal by talking with people, listening to their stories with an open mind; ready to use their information as we reformulate our opinions. At 79 years old, my father possesses a far greater wealth of knowledge and experience than I have, three times over, and I would be a fool if I ignored that. Also, I would be as arrogant as can be if I thought my opinions immutable.

Likewise, my father knows I am a newshound for alternative media, and he is interested in the information I find there as well as the information I glean from talking with others. He who cannot change his mind likely does not possess one, and I can only hope I am as open-minded as my father is at his age.

Watching the mainstream media, one might think civil society in this country is dead. However, beneath the surface there is growing political discourse. People are now asking questions about the war. People are reading the Constitution and wondering about the PATRIOT Act. People are talking with each other. Maybe they are no longer feeling so alone. Maybe they are seeing that democracy is fragile and that it requires much more maintenance than simply voting and then going home, watching television, surfing the net, and buying stuff.

These are things my father also knows and he knows something has gone wrong in Iraq. Another basic moral principle is that you are responsible for the consequences of your actions and inactions. We are responsible for what we have wrought upon Iraq, and every day it becomes, to paraphrase Donald Rumsfeld, a more untidy mess, one that appears to be spreading to non-Iraqi militants who are entering the fray to fight U.S. soldiers.

The conflict is also spreading beyond Iraq. Other governments are following our lead in dealing with people whom they disagree with and excusing their actions as part of the war on terror even as their actions are simply terror.[6]

Of all the things my father knows, he knows that we do not have all the answers. The goal of a free society is not to know all the answers, but one in which everyone has a say in coming up with the answers, and if we make mistakes, we have an obligation to correct them. The world is not black and white. Humans are complex creatures and answers to our questions, queries, problems, trials, tribulations, and temptations are not easily found and will remain unanswerable if we do not engage them with others.

My father is now 79 years old. Many years have passed since he risked his life and did his best to pass on the ideals of this country. Thirty-four years have passed since he began sharing his beliefs with me. His hearing is going and so, too, he claims, is his memory. Regardless, he is a wealth of information and wisdom, and I value every conversation I have with him, whether on the phone or the two or three times a year I make it home.

If I have children one day I may find myself thinking just like him—in a practical manner. I can only hope that whether or not I espouse such practicality, I give my children half the love he and my mother have always given my brother and me in setting such a fine example.

Democracy and freedom are fragile to be sure. Our country's institutions have proved resilient over the years because of people like my father; those I know from Portland's Jobs with

Justice; the activists at the Portland Central America Solidarity Committee; the janitors of SEIU Local 49; the Longshoremen at ILWU Locals 4, 5, and 8; the nurses at Providence-Milwaukie Hospital; the workers at Williams Controls; the booksellers at Powell's City of Books, and hundreds of thousands of others about whom you and I will never hear, who fought to preserve and augment our institutions so people like you and I could lead better lives. They stood up against those who would usurp these treasured institutions and use them for their own selfish purposes. These heroes are not George Washington, Abraham Lincoln, or Franklin Delano Roosevelt. They aren't even Emma Goldman, Eugene Debs, or Dorothy Day.

You will likely never read about these wonderful people in your textbooks, but you can meet and talk with them every day on the street. The choice is ours. We can talk with people, attend meetings, and constantly assess and, as needed, reassess our position in society and act upon our convictions. Or we can just get information from the mainstream-managed news sources and sit at home, not interacting with the outer world beyond playing video games and surfing the internet. The first option may very well amount to nothing, but the second only better assures that things get worse.

Yesterday I spoke with my dad. Somehow the old codger, who was born in Brooklyn, once home to the Dodgers, has come to root for the Yankees in the World Series. Such behavior would have been deemed sacrilegious not long ago, and if my mother's mother were still alive, she would have some harsh words for my father. Time has mellowed my father, and he better appreciates the art of baseball; or maybe I have finally learned what he always appreciated in the game.

We also talked about Iraq. At least, he told me, the right thing happened. He was referring to Saddam no longer being in power.

The right thing? We are purportedly spreading democracy, while telling the Iraqi people that our interests are their interests and that their government will reflect this. We have thrown international law out the window, committing crimes for which Nazis were hanged. Thousands of Iraqis have been killed. American soldiers are being killed and many more are being injured every day. Countries are realizing the best way to avoid being invaded by the United States is to get real weapons of mass destruction.

More and more countries that provided goodwill toward the United States in the days following 9/11 now find our country reckless. Osama bin Laden is still at large. Al Qaeda is regrouping. As $87 billion—not in one iota marked for reparations—heads to Iraq, our schools are falling apart, people are losing their jobs and health insurance, and in the wealthiest country in the world, too many people are living in the abject misery of poverty.

Indeed, some positive things have happened in Iraq,[7] including Saddam being thrown out of power and subsequently captured. However, we must also consider how we achieve the ends, for they do not always justify the means, and my list of wrongs is far longer and, I think, of greater magnitude than the positives my father sees.

Because I talk about the situation in Iraq with my father and neither of us has all day, we only focus on a few of the problems. After all, there are others to talk with as well. Not talk at, or to, but with.

FOOTNOTES

1   For information regarding the number of people in Iraq who have died as a result of UN sanctions, see Matthew Rothschild's interview with Former UN Humanitarian Coordinator Denis Halliday, *The Progressive*, 63:2, February 1999, 26. Available at <http://consistentlife.org/Denis%20Halliday%20Interview.htm>. Halliday stated the death toll is probably closer now to 600,000 and that is over the period of 1990–1998. If you include adults, it is well over 1 million Iraqi people. Also, according to a United Nations Children's Fund (UNICEF) report, the mortality rate of children under five years old had more than doubled since

sanctions were levied on Iraq in 1991 (Iraq Survey Shows Humanitarian Emergency, August 12, 1999. Available at <http://www.unicef.org/newsline/99pr29.htm>. For a more comprehensive list of links regarding the sanctions see <http://www.betterworldlinks.org/book60g.htm>.

2   See Eric Rouleau, "The View from France: America's Unyielding Policy toward Iraq," *Foreign Affairs*, Vol. 74, No. 1, January/February 1995.

3   For an interesting and important study that reveals why a substantial portion of the public had a number of misconceptions that were demonstrably false or at odds with the dominant view in the intelligence community see http://www.pipa.org/OnlineReports/Iraq/Media_10_02_03_Report.pdf.

4   For a quiz that reveals how many countries became democracies as a result of U.S. bombing since the end of World War II, see <http://www.zmag.org/content/showarticle.cfm?SectionID=15&Item ID=3141>.

5   See <http://www.globenet.free-online.co.uk/articles/ourally.htm>.

6   For just a small taste of how terror has spread beyond Iraq, see how Russia is dealing with Chechnyans, and how union organizers at Coca-Cola's Colombian bottling plants are kidnapped, tortured, and murdered by paramilitary groups often allegedly working closely with plant management (see: www.killercoke.org). Consider the ideas available at Democracy Now! September 17, 2003. The transcript is available at <http://www.democracynow.org/article.pl?sid=03/09/17/1543215.

7   For more information regarding how money is spent in Iraq, see just about any article by Naomi Klein (author of the fabulous *No Logo*). For starters, see her "Risky Business" available at http://www.thenation.com/doc.mhtml?i=20040105&s=klein&c=1; and "Bring Halliburton Home" available at http://www.thenation.com/doc.mhtml?i=20031124&s=klein. Also available from Alternative Radio is her talk "Economic Warfare: From Argentina to Iraq." Available for purchase at www.alternativeradio.org.

■ Essay Ten ■

SILENT VOICES

Terrance L. Furin, Ph.D.

Assistant Professor of Education,
Saint Joseph's University

If we are to get on with our more than 200-year-old experiment in strengthening democracy we need to have more participation from 18–21-year-old Americans. Only as they choose to get involved, as they realize how vital it is that they learn about matters like our current involvement in Iraq—and its many implications for THEIR future—can we hope to have an informed electorate provide the ever-better guidance that challenges like the Second Gulf War pose. The stakes could not be higher. Can you help get more young people involved?—Editor

---

WHISPERS

Presidential elections are a chance for Americans to whisper softly or give full voice as to who will lead our country for four years. The debate for the 2004 election has increasingly focused on the Iraq War. Budget deficits have soared, and American lives have been lost almost daily since the president declared on May 2, 2003, aboard the USS *Abraham Lincoln*, that "major combat operations in Iraq have ended."[1]

In 2000, Americans *whispered*, and, by the *slimmest of*

margins, George W. Bush became the 43rd President of the United States. *Whispered* because only 51.3 percent of the voting-age population cast their ballots. *Slimmest of margins* because the president actually received less than the majority of popular votes cast—50,456,002 out of 104,338,854.[2] This made the 2000 election the closest of the past century, eclipsing the 1960 race between John Kennedy and Richard Nixon.[3]

Most disturbing about the 2000 election *whisper* is that two-thirds of younger voters (defined as 18–24-year-olds) did not vote.[4] Yet this is the age-group that has been called upon to fight the Iraq War, and the very people who are most affected by staggering deficits that borrow on the future. This disengagement is reminiscent of another time, approximately 35 years ago, when America's young voices also were not heard. They, however, went from silence to affecting our nation's history in many important ways.

"SOUNDS OF SILENCE": AN AGE OF DISCONTENT

The 1967 Mike Nichols movie *The Graduate* depicts a time of disenfranchisement and estrangement of American youth. One of the songs popularized by the movie, Paul Simon's "Sounds of Silence," captures the mood of a generation with words such as " ... ten thousand people, maybe more ... talking without speaking ... hearing without listening."[5] The late 1960s and early '70s were times when our nation's conscience was bared before the world. It was a time filled with more questions than answers—a time of confusion, torment, and pain.

Many American youth wanted a say in politics at this time because they were the ones fighting a war that had divided the nation. Eighteen-year-old men could be drafted into the armed forces yet could not vote until age 21. After registering at 18, local draft boards would decide whether a man had to report for duty or would be granted a deferment for reasons such as poor health, enrollment in college, or entrance into a critical profession such as teaching. This deferment system led to many inequities and was replaced by a national lottery on December 1, 1969.

The lottery was a roulette-like gamble with lives. All days in the year were drawn and placed on a chart that determined if a man would be drafted into service. If you had a low number (below 195) chances were good that you would have to go as there were very few deferments (If you want to see how your birthday matches with the lottery numbers go to www.cnn.com/SPECIALS/cold.war/episodes/13/the.draft/ and enter your birth month and day.)

The Vietnam War filled many young people with a rage that was especially evident on American college and university campuses. This rage erupted into violence following President Nixon's April 30, 1970, decision to expand the war by invading Vietnam's neighbor Cambodia.[6] The violence led to a tragically sad chapter in our history when U.S. troops actually shot and killed American students at Kent State University in Ohio.[7]

I will never forget the deep anguish expressed by students in my high school U.S. history classes following the shootings at Kent State on May 4, 1970. Located less than an hour from our large suburban high school, Kent State was the university of choice for many of our graduates and teachers. We simply could not believe that U.S. soldiers had shot and killed American citizens so close to our homes. This event crystallized emotions and made history come alive for our students who determined that their voices would be heard.

WHEN YOUNG VOICES WERE HEARD

The war became a focus for real discussions throughout the school as students staged walkouts, protests, and peace rallies. They also began to express strong views on other serious issues such as racial hatred, urban blight, the country's uncontrolled consumption of natural resources, and severe damage to the world environment. Discussions on most of these issues were more relevant than the social studies curriculum that was taught from outdated textbooks. Mental exercises, such as memorizing the "four causes of the War of 1812" (in order of importance), seemed far removed from social problems affecting students who were living in the present.

Administrators and teachers in our school district felt a similar disconnection and, with student input, we redesigned the entire 7–12th grade social studies curriculum to include numerous nine-week courses centered upon topics such as "dissent and democracy," "war and peace," "crisis in urban America," "black history," and "minority struggle." The courses were interdisciplinary and created lively learning based on materials such as relevant paperback books, multimedia presentations, outside speakers, and numerous field trips.

Students still had to meet their two years of required social studies courses but were now permitted choices. Interest in social studies grew dramatically. Many chose to take electives beyond the two-year requirement. In fact, overall enrollment in various social studies courses grew by more than 20 percent.

Ironically, the end of the Vietnam War coupled with some improvement in civil rights, led to a decline in student activism. This, in turn, resulted in the death of these innovations and the reemergence of a traditional curriculum controlled by texts and built primarily on survey courses in world history, U.S. history, and U.S. government. However, one major change for young adults remains to this day—the 26th Amendment to the Constitution, which lowered the voting age from 21 to 18.

"SOUNDS OF SILENCE" ONCE AGAIN

It was hoped that with the passage of this amendment American youth would find a greater voice in American politics. Instead, according to several national organizations, the decline in participation for young voters has increased steadily.[8] In analyzing the fact that two-thirds of the younger voters did not vote in the 2000 election, an article in the *Carnegie Reporter* states that "... it is the youth vote that quadrennially absorbs most anxieties about our democracy's future health."[9]

Some of the reasons for lack of interest may lie in the fact that social studies education is not considered very important today. The Bush administration's new federal "No Child Left Behind" legislation does not include social studies among the nationally tested subjects. Reporting on a recent meeting of

7,000 middle and high school students in Maryland, *Baltimore Sun* correspondent Mike Bowler wrote that the new federal law requires yearly testing in math and reading but not in social studies. A social studies coordinator at the meeting stated, "if it ain't tested, it ain't taught ... I hate to say it but it's true."[10] Others agree with this assessment. Cynthia Gibson of the Carnegie Corporation is quoted in the *Boston Globe* as saying that civics education has been "placed on the back burner."[11]

Not stressing history, government, and other social studies education is only part of the problem. Time and again I hear from recent high school graduates that the social studies—especially history and civics—are their least favorite and most boring subjects. I believe that one of the main reasons for this is that adults—especially those in positions of power—do not know how to communicate with youth. We know how to debate and produce winners and losers. We know how to lecture, oftentimes with arrogance and impatience. We do not, however, develop dialogue in which listening, reflecting, and sharing lead to deep understandings. The result is a new generation of silent voices.

VOICES OF DIALOGUE

Phi Delta Kappan, a professional journal for educators, dedicated a special section of its September 2003 issue to "democracy and civic engagement." In one article, Joseph Kahne and Joel Westheimer state that "... citizens [and particularly young citizens] are often disengaged from politics" while at the same time "more than 24 million young Americans cast votes to elect an 'American Idol.'"[12] In this same journal, Timothy J. Stanley writes that "democracy cannot survive unless people come together in dialogue to develop shared projects despite differences and without unduly imposing their conceptions of the good life on others ... after all, the past is littered with efforts that started with the noblest of intentions—only to end in tyranny."[13]

In hopes of developing greater political engagement among our young citizens, the magazine lists 29 model organizations and projects. One of these, in particular, is aimed at creating student empowerment through dialogue on student issues. It is called "Project 540" and is funded by the Pew Charitable Trusts through Providence College. In describing the project, *Phi Delta Kappan* editors write that it "gives students nation-wide the opportunity to talk about issues that matter to them and to turn these conversations into real school and community change."[14] (You can click on the Project 540 Web site to explore this interesting project for yourself: www.project540.com.)

I discussed "Project 540" recently with Dr. Harris Sokoloff of the University of Pennsylvania, who has developed several "540" initiatives over the past two years. In more than 22 different schools in the Philadelphia region, students have engaged in dialogues through which they identify a range of issues and action plans to address problems. Some of these have included the quality of cafeteria food or the conditions of bathrooms. Others go well beyond these physical issues. One program, for example, concentrated on a run-down high school and led to the formation of a citizens' committee to renovate the school. Another project involves high school students working with graduate students from the University of Pennsylvania to redesign a waterfront area.

MORE THAN USELESS?
The future well-being of our democracy depends on all of us becoming engaged with the issues that we face. Pericles, an ancient Greek leader, spoke directly about the vitality of Athenian democracy when he said "... regarding him who takes no part in [public matters] not as unambitious but as useless."[15] Most certainly, we need to be more than useless.

As Pericles knew, democracies are fragile political systems that need to be continuously nourished through active citizen participation. This is especially true for our youth as they are the future of our democracy. It is through dialogue that ideas take shape and voiceless individuals become empowered. It is through dialogue, to paraphrase Paul Simon, that "... ten thousand people, maybe more ..." can talk while speaking and listen while hearing. The best defense a democracy has against the evils of despotism is for silent voices to be heard. We desperately need to hear them now.

FOOTNOTES

1 "Bush Calls End to Major Combat," CNN.com/world, 2 May 2003, accessed 28 October 2003: <http://www.cnn.com/2003/world/meast/05/01/sprj.irq.main/>.
2 The "popular votes" for the three major candidates were as follows: George W. Bush—50,456,002; Albert A. Gore—50,999,897; Ralph Nader—2,882,955. The "electoral vote," which is determined by the constitutional provision for an electoral college, is based upon each state's number of senators and representatives and favored Bush as follows: George W. Bush—271, Albert A. Gore—266, Ralph Nader—0. If you want to see for yourself, this information was gathered from this Web site: <http://www.infoplease.com/ipa/A0781450.html on October 18, 2003>.
3 In 1960, John F. Kennedy received 34,226,731 popular votes and 303 electoral votes compared with Richard Nixon's 34,108,157 popular votes and 219 electoral votes. This information was gathered from the same Web site as the prior footnote.
4 "The Youth Vote," *Carnegie Reporter*, Carnegie Corporation of New York, Vol. 1/No. 2, Spring 2001, accessed 4 March 2003: <http://www.Carnegie.org/reporter/02/vote2000/vote.html>.
5 Paul Simon, "Sounds of Silence," CD insert, *Simon & Garfunkel, Sounds of Silence*, New York: Sony Music Entertainment, 1997.
6 Concluding a nationally televised speech explaining his decision, Nixon said, in words that are eerily similar to those of George W. Bush's defense of his Iraq War decisions: "My fellow Americans, we live in an age of anarchy, both abroad and at home ... If, when the chips are down, the world's most powerful nation, the United States of America, acts like a pitiful, helpless giant, the forces of totalitarianism and anarchy will threaten free nations and free institutions throughout the world." "President Nixon's Speech on Cambodia, April 30, 1970," 30 April 1970, accessed 21 October 2003: <http://vietnam.vassar.edu/doc15.html>.

7   Kent State University maintains excellent archives, many that include pictures. They are available on the Internet at <http://speccoll.library.kent.edu/4may70/>.

8   For more information see the following Web sites: <www.stateofthevote.org>; <www.civicyouth.org>.

9   "The Youth Vote," *Carnegie Reporter*, Carnegie Corporation of New York, Vol. 1/No. 2, Spring 2001, accessed 4 March 2003: <http://www.Carnegie.org/reporter/02/vote2000/vote.html>.

10 Mike Bowler, "Teachers Fear Social Studies Is Becoming History; State Tests Are Cutting Time for Subject They Say," *Baltimore Sun*, 6 May 2003: <http://web.lexis-nexis.com/universe/printdoc>.

11 Karla Kingsley, *Boston Globe*, 16 March 2003, accessed 16 March 2003: <http://www.boston.com/dailyglobe2/075/1...es_mirros_decline_in_youth_voteP.shtml>.

12 Joseph Kahne and Joel Westheimer, "Teaching Democracy: What Schools Need to Do," *Phi Delta Kappan*, September 2003, 35.

13 Kahne and Westheimer, 38.

14 Kahne and Westheimer, 67.

15 Thucydides, "Book II, Pericles' Funeral Oration," *The History of the Peloponnesian War*, 22 September 2002: <http://www.mtholyoke.edu/acad/intrel/pericles.htm>.

■ Essay Eleven ■

WHAT CAN AND SHOULD WE DO—AND WHY?

R. Dean Wright, Ph.D.

Ellis and Nelle Levitt Professor of Sociology,
Drake University

If you opposed the Second Gulf War before it
began, what might your position be now? Why?
And with what implications for personal sacrifice, for helping to pay the bill, and for helping to
guide Iraq's recovery?—Editor

We can, and probably will, debate the question of whether we
should have invaded Iraq and whether we should withdraw
long into our future. The fact is that we did invade Iraq and
today the issue becomes what to do now that we are there.

Between the first U.S.-Iraq war, more than a decade ago, and
today, the society, culture, and social-psychology of the nation
and its people have all but been destroyed. There is now a moral
obligation on our part to put it back together as much as possible and assist Iraq and its people in becoming a stable society.

As our government ponders its future steps, we can see many
parallels with how we have approached wartime during past
centuries. It is often said that we seldom learn the lessons that
history teaches. However, when it comes to the issue of how we
should deal with other nations once war is over, the lesson is
clear. Hatred for other nations, their way of life, or their
leaders is immense during the time of war. We have to have

enemies, figureheads, whether real or perceived as real, that we can point to as the symbol of that evil.

England, Japan, Italy, Germany, Russia, China, and a host of other cultures have, at one time or another, been an enemy of the United States. Yet, not long after the conflict had ended, they became our allies; each with strong ties to the United States.

The parallel with these past wars and disputes is abundantly clear. With this historical parallel, we have a clear pathway that we must take. Today, the United States has a moral obligation to put back together, as much as possible, the nation that modern technology allowed us to quickly destroy. We must now make available to the people of Iraq all those resources they need to be mended.

In his book *The Conquerors: Roosevelt, Truman and the Destruction of Hitler's Germany*, Michael Beschloss provides us with a remarkable parallel set of decisions that were made at the conclusion of World War II. Many advisors to President Franklin Roosevelt, especially Secretary of the Treasury Henry Morgenthau, recommended that the United States totally destroy the capacity of Germany to rebuild itself following the war. He, and those supporting his viewpoint, wanted to bomb Germany back into an agrarian society. Roosevelt was never fully persuaded by the arguments, noting that such behavior was an antithesis of the tradition of the United States.

Roosevelt died before World War II ended, allowing the new president, Harry Truman, to listen to his own advisors. The rest is history. The Marshall Plan and other programs set forth a blueprint whereby Europe was rebuilt and given the opportunity to construct its own future. Almost 60 years later Germany, Italy, and Japan have matured into strong nations that are no longer focused on world domination. Even though city after city was in ruins following World War II, there is little evidence today of that war in modern Europe.

The maturity of these nations that were once our bitter enemies was recently demonstrated by the independence of Germany in its refusal to side with the United States during the invasion of Iraq. Although Germany recognizes and appreciates the role the United States played in its rebirth, it refuses to follow in lockstep with the pathway taken by the United States. The war carried out by the United States has essentially left Iraq in a condition not unlike what existed in Germany, Italy, and Japan following World War II. Although rebuilding Iraq will require an immense amount of economic and personal capital, the same reality that the United States faced in the mid-1940s does exist. It will take a long time to create conditions that will give Iraq the opportunity to chart its own pathway toward whatever form its society and culture takes. The depth of the cultural clash between Iraq and the United States makes it impossible for Iraq to adopt the same model of government that was possible in Europe and Japan following World War II.

Iraq, as well as many other nations in that region of the world, is theocratic. Theocratic cultures, governments, and legal systems cannot travel down the same pathway as that taken by the United States, where the separation of religion and state is an ironclad rule. We cannot create a duplicate of the United States in Iraq, and we would be unwise to try to force that to happen. Iraq, and most of the Middle East, must be assisted in charting its own future and moving in its own direction. The United States now has a moral obligation to see that Iraq is rebuilt in the most humane manner possible and with the greatest dispatch.

The history of the Middle East is filled with wars, conflict, and colonialism. Countless centuries of conquest and domination have left a deep resentment toward ruling nations. This is an inevitable consequence of power being used against those less powerful. Look around the world and you will find example after example of this reality.

This resentment runs deep, just as the resentment held by many Southerners toward Northerners in the United States is partly a consequence of a war that took place in the middle of the nineteenth century. Modern Southerners never knew the pains of Sherman's march on Atlanta, but the scars left by that war are still felt by many residents who reside in that region.

I wrote a couple of pieces before the invasion of Iraq in

which I declared my opposition to the war. I still think that we were ill-prepared for the war as well as the complex set of consequences that followed and will continue into the future.

However, now that the United States selected its course of action we need to deal with reality. It will take decades before the scars left by the wars with Iraq heal. The United States now faces a moral obligation to do what it can to secure the area and provide for a smooth transition of the nation back to its own people. Only through strong leadership, planning, and commitment can that happen.

The time is here for the United States to live up to the words that our founders set down in the documents that led to our own independence. We must be a nation that respects the rights of all peoples to their own pursuit of life, liberty, and happiness.

REFERENCE

Beschloss, Michael. *The Conquerors: Roosevelt, Truman and the Destruction of Hitler's Germany*. New York: Simon & Schuster, 2002.

BLOOD FOR OIL? GULF WAR II AND THE "ULTIMATE STRATEGIC PETROLEUM RESERVE"

Benjamin Liebman, Ph.D.

Assistant Professor of Economics,
Saint Joseph's University

If we are not to go to war over oil supplies, we must rapidly and significantly reduce our reliance on imported fossil fuels. We must get MUCH better at substituting such renewable fuels as biomass, hydro, hydrogen, nuclear, solar, thermal, tidal, wave, and wind, etc., for oil and domestic coal. We must improve conservation in 101 ways, such as redesigning our traffic patterns. Congestion annually wastes billions of gallons of fuel. We must improve the mpg rate of our car and truck fleet, and we must win converts to walking and bicycle and train use. Otherwise, our ever-greater "addiction" to imported oil may "drive" our foreign affairs in ways dangerous to everyone.—Editor

---

Many opponents of the U.S.-led effort to topple Saddam Hussein believe the war was fought to grant U.S. and British oil companies better access to Iraq's vast oil wealth, or in the very least, facilitate a change in regime that would better serve the U.S. economy's enormous demand for oil.

A good place to start an analysis here is by noting that in

2001, Iraq supplied ONLY about 7 percent of U.S. petroleum imports, or about 4 percent of total U.S. petroleum consumption. Skeptics of the "blood-for-oil" theory point out that this is simply not enough oil to justify a war, even for the most adamant supporters of a petroleum-based economy.

Of course, removing Saddam Hussein could make the entire Persian Gulf a safer, more stable neighborhood. Since 23 percent of U.S. oil imports stem from this region, removing such an unpredictable, aggressive autocrat could certainly help protect multiple suppliers of U.S. energy.

Finally, Iraq is a member of OPEC (Organization of Petroleum Exporting Countries), a group of nations that cooperate with one another by limiting their exports in order to keep world oil prices at suitably profitable levels. OPEC produces approximately 40 percent of the world's oil, and contains seven of the world's top ten biggest exporters. It supplies almost half of all U.S. oil imports—an undoubtedly significant portion of the United State's total energy demand (see Table 1).

As the United States gets more than half of its oil from non-OPEC countries, it is reasonable to ask why we are so vulnerable to OPEC's policies. The answer to this question is one of the most critical factors in the world oil market: the supply of oil is kept fairly close to the demand for oil, so that even if a minor import source is threatened, there will be a sudden shortfall.

However, there is one way that a sudden shortfall in world supply will NOT lead to a large and extended rise in oil prices. Saudi Arabia has the unique ability to quickly and cheaply increase its output on a massive scale. For this reason, it possesses what some observers call the "oil weapon," whereby it can cut production and unleash havoc on the world economy, or, instead, quickly increase production and stabilize the world economy.

With over a quarter of the world's proven reserves, Saudi Arabia's leadership in the world oil market remains unchallenged (see Table 2). Accordingly, some experts believe that the real threat of Saddam Hussein prior to the first Gulf War stemmed not from his control over Iraq's oil but rather his ability to invade Saudi Arabia, as well as Kuwait and the UAE, and thereby take control of more than 55 percent of the world's oil reserves.

From a strategic standpoint, therefore, removing Saddam Hussein could help ensure continued access to the majority of the world's proven oil reserves. The importance of such access was expressed by General Anthony Zinni, Commander in Chief, U.S. Central Command, who testified before Congress that the Gulf Region, with its huge oil reserves, is a "vital interest" of "long standing" for the United States and that the United States "must have free access to the region's resources."[1]

However, Iraq's importance to the world energy market lies not just in its proven reserves or even its proximity to Saudi Arabia, Kuwait, and the UAE. The real economic significance of Iraq is not simply in its sizable proven reserves or even its critical geographic location. Its ultimate strategic value rests in the fact that it may contain more oil than any other country on the planet.

And this potential will become increasingly important as oil wells in the United States and abroad run dry over the next 40 years. As Vice President Dick Cheney said in 1999, "On our present course, America 20 years from now will import nearly two out of every three barrels of oil—a condition of increased dependency on foreign powers that do not always have America's interest at heart."[2]

If Iraq was able to bring its production up to its true capacity—possibly 8 million barrels per day—it could replace Saudi Arabia as the guarantor of world supplies. With this kind of output alongside an Iraqi regime more closely allied to the United States, "the oil weapon is neutralized," says Dr. F.J. Chalabi.[3]

Even more optimistically, a former Iraqi deputy oil minister states that, "It is not necessarily easy, but the scenario exists whereby Britain and the United States, by handling Iraq's oil resources a certain way, could carve out the ultimate 'strategic petroleum reserve.' It is certainly feasible."[4] With potentially insurmountable opposition from environmentalists over drilling in Alaska's Arctic National Wildlife Reserve (estimated 16 billion barrels), such a scenario becomes even more attractive.

Thus, despite the fact that Iraq supplied a relatively minor share of U.S. oil imports (7 percent) just prior to the war, its potential to support the United State's enormous petroleum demand in the future cannot be overstressed.

Policy makers closely connected to the energy industry would, of course, be especially cognizant of the long-run benefits of replacing a hostile Iraqi regime with a friendly one. Indeed, much has been made of the close connections between President Bush's administration and the U.S. oil industry. Financial disclosure forms reveal that the top 100 officials in the Bush administration have the majority of their personal investments in traditional energy and natural resource sectors.[5]

How exactly are U.S. corporate oil interests served by removing Saddam Hussein? First, while Persian Gulf countries have the majority of the world's reserves, the technology and facilities required to develop, transport, and refine this oil belong to the world's industrial giants. For example, the United States alone refines about 17 mbd, while all of OPEC refines less than 8 mbd (or about 11 percent of the world total).[6]

However, despite their dominance in shipping and processing the world's oil, the giant U.S., British, and French multinational oil companies are still forced to buy much of their oil on the open market from OPEC members.

Some experts believe that as it becomes increasingly expensive to replace reserves in non-OPEC areas, future profits will depend on whether the multinationals can gain control, or at least production-sharing rights, to reserves located in new sources.[7] Presently, the nationalized oil industries in Saudi Arabia, Kuwait, and Venezuela remain off limits. Fadel Gheit, an investment specialist, has written that Iraq "would be a logical place in the future for oil companies to replace their reserves."[8]

A critical development prior to war was that Saddam had been negotiating with French, Russian, and Chinese oil companies to develop Iraq's immense but relatively untapped oil fields. Some observers believe an underlying motive of the war was to jeopardize these French, Russian, and Chinese contracts, and renew hopes that U.S. and British multinationals could gain a stake in the development of Iraqi oil.

As Credit Suisse First Boston Oil analyst Mark Flannery said: "If you turn up and it's your tanks that dislodge the regime, and you have 50,000 troops in the country, and they're in your tanks, then you're going to get the best deals." [9]

In light of the fact that the war has indeed jeopardized these lucrative contracts with Russia, France, and China, perhaps the United States and Great Britain faced a win-win situation in their unrelenting drive to invade Iraq. If France, Russia, and China chose to join the U.S.-led coalition, the financial and military burdens of the war would be shared. On the other hand, if the United States and Great Britain were forced to go it alone, U.S. and British multinationals would then be in the best position to establish new contracts to develop Iraq's oil.

This in no way suggests that the administration believed developing Iraq's oil would be easy or costless. A U.S. Department of Energy analysis prior to the war determined that rebuilding Iraq's oil industry would be fraught with difficulties. These included: 1) dealing with the current poor state of Iraq's infrastructure; 2) the need for repairs and restoration of oil production and export installation facilities estimated at $10 billion; and 3) the threat of damage to Iraq's oil facilities due to sabotage and general unrest. The consensus was that a "bonanza" of oil should not be expected out of Iraq anytime in the near future.

This notwithstanding, at the outset of the war, the U.S. was faced with two promising scenarios with regard to Iraq's oil. In the first, U.S. companies receive a substantial portion of the fantastic profits—estimated at more than $3 trillion dollars—that awaits the producer of Iraq's reserves. [10]

In a second scenario, U.S. multinationals might fail to secure a share in the production of Iraq's vast oil wealth (most likely because Washington would fear appearing overly imperialistic to the Iraqi people), but the war nevertheless leads to a potentially democratic Iraq with stronger ties to Washington.

This, in turn, helps secure the future supply of the United States' increasing thirst for oil and reduces the possibility of disruptions to world oil markets.

In the words of one State Department official: "At the end of the day, all the talk of a 'carve-up' is overheated. Suffice it to say, the U.S. would be satisfied to see Iraq emerge as a democracy, and democracies are not something you generally find in OPEC."[11]

Ultimately, however, the existence of these potential benefits to oil corporations and the U.S. (petroleum-based) economy does not necessarily imply that the war was fought over oil. Instead, it may simply indicate that U.S. corporate and/or general (long-run) economic interest could be served by simultaneously fulfilling the stated goal of the war—removing a brutal, repressive dictator who was no longer willing to prove to international inspectors that he wasn't stockpiling the chemical weapons he had used on his own people a decade before.

FOOTNOTES

1   James A. Paul, "Oil in Iraq: the Heart of the Crisis." Global Policy Forum. Available at <http://globalpolicy.org/security/oil/2002/12heart.htm>.

2   Alex Johnson, "U.S. Politics: Is the Fix In?" 10 September 2003. Available at <http://www.msnbc.com/news/823985.asp?0cb=-515114700>.

3   Michael Moran, "The Saudis: Between Iraq and..." 10 September 2003. Available at <http://www.msnbc.com/news/823985.asp?0cb=-415114700>.

4   Michael Moran and Alex Johnson, "Oil: The Other Iraq War." 10 September 2003. Available at <http://www.msnbc.com/news/823985.asp?0cb=-115114700>.

5   Ibid.

6   See <http://www.opec.org>.

7   Paul, "Oil in Iraq: the Heart of the Crisis."

8   Ibid.

9 John W. Schoen, "Iraqi Oil, American Bonanza." 10 September
   2003. Available at
   <http://www.msnbc.com/news/823985.asp?0cb=-315114700>.
10 James A. Paul, "Iraq: the Struggle for Oil." Global Policy Forum.
   Available at <http://globalpolicy.org/security/oil/2002/08jim.htm>.
11 Alex Johnson, "U.S. Politics: Is the Fix In?" 10 September 2003.
   Available at
   <http://www.msnbc.com/news/823985.asp?0cb=-515114700>.

REFERENCES

Derr, Kenneth T. "Engagement—A Better Alternative." 5 November
   1998. Chevron Speech Archives. Available at
   <http://www.chevrontexaco.com/news/archive/chevron_speech/
   1998/98-11-05.asp>.
Iraq Country Analysis Brief. Available at <http://www.eia.doe.gov/
   emeu/cabs/iraq.html>.
Lieber, Robert J. *The Oil Decade: Conflict and Cooperation in the West.*
   Lanham, Md.: Rowman & Littlefield, 1986.
_____. "Iraq and the World Oil Markets" in *Iraq's Road to War.* Edited
   by Amatzia Baram and Barry Rubin. New York: St. Martin's Press,
   1993.
U.S. Department of Energy, Energy Information Administration.
   Available at <http://www.eia.doe.gov/>.
Yergin, Daniel. "Crisis and Adjustment: An Overview" in Daniel
   Yergin and Martin Hellenbrand, eds., *Global Insecurity: A Strategy
   for Energy and Economic Renewal.* Boston, Mass: Houghton Mifflin
   Press, 1982.

TABLES

Table 1. Top World Net Oil Exporters (2002) (OPEC members in italics)

Export Source	Net Oil Exports (mbd)
Saudi Arabia	7.00
Russia	5.03
Norway	3.14
Venezuela	2.46
Iran	2.26
UAE	2.07
Nigeria	1.85
Kuwait	1.73
Mexico	1.68
Iraq	1.58
Algeria	1.34
Libya	1.17

[Source: U.S. Department of Energy/Energy Information Administration]

Table 2. Greatest Oil Reserves by Country (millions of barrels, 2002)

Country	Proven Reserves	Percent of World Reserves
Saudi Arabia	261,750	25.4
Iraq	112,500	10.9
UAE	97,800	9.5
Kuwait	96,500	9.4
Iran	89,700	8.7
Venezuela	77,685	7.5
Russia	48,573	4.7
Libya	29,500	2.9
Mexico	26,941	2.6
Nigeria	24,000	2.3
China	24,000	2.3
United States	22,045	2.1
Rest of the World	56,983	5.5
OPEC	845,412	78.7
World	1,032,132	

[Source: http://www.thirdworldtraveler.com/Oil_watch/World_Oil%20_Table.html]

■ Essay Thirteen ■

FIGHTING FEAR TO SECURE THE FUTURE

Lane Jennings, Ph.D.

Production Editor, *Future Survey*

Imagine the situation in Iraq today if the U.S.-led Coalition had not forced a change in regime. Imagine what might happen if we withdraw with much left unachieved. All the more vital, therefore, is the effort to see Iraqis create the quality of constitution that could show the way in the Middle East to a Grand Muslim Renaissance, a surge in freedom, well-being, and peace greater than any known to date.—Editor

---

Both supporters and critics of "The War on Terrorism" generally offer political or economic motives to explain U.S. policies and actions. This essay considers recent events in the light of two cultural factors: fear and the future.[1]

FIGHTING A CRIME, NOT A CULTURE

In American eyes, the hijackings and mass murders of September 11, 2001, look more like acts of criminal insanity than military strikes. Consequently, the U.S. response has resembled a crime investigation more than total mobilization for war. Government officials and opinion leaders alike have stressed repeatedly that the United States has no desire to permanently occupy a foreign nation, much less to destroy Islam. We are fighting terrorism—the use of indiscriminate violence to spread fear and disrupt daily life—practiced by any group, for any motive, anywhere.

In a criminal investigation, much of the work remains unpublicized. So, too, much of the War on Terrorism is waged quietly in offices and laboratories, banks and archives. The highly visible but limited military actions in Afghanistan and Iraq contribute to our overall goal by denying facilities, free movement, and supplies to groups and individuals who had clearly demonstrated that they both practiced and supported terrorist acts. To judge our progress solely by battle reports and casualty counts, though, is like rating the merits of a criminal prosecution by how easily police SWAT teams flush out the suspects.[2]

FEAR ITSELF

Imagine for a moment that the invasion of Iraq never took place. What would be different today?

Inside Iraq, Saddam Hussein would still be ruling, secure in the expectation that his sons Qusay and Uday would one day succeed him. Iraq's minority populations would still be forcibly prevented from living and worshipping as they choose. Under Baath Party control, every Iraqi would still live in constant fear of arbitrary arrest, imprisonment, and torture. UN sanctions would still be in force constraining the economy. Iraq's oil wealth would still enrich a few individuals, not benefit the nation as a whole.

If Saddam Hussein were still in power, the nations bordering Iraq, some with painful memories of past invasions, would still have reason to fear new attacks. UN arms inspectors might still be at work, turning up a banned missile here, a suspicious clue there, but never able—because never permitted—to prove conclusively that Iraq could NOT unleash deadly force on targets far outside its borders.

Above all, if there had been no invasion, many would suspect (but never know) what quantities of weapons, funds, and other help might still be flowing every day from Iraq to support terrorist operations throughout the world. Nations would fear Iraq's potential, yet remain unable to judge the justification of those fears. Some, expecting the worst, would take costly precautions; others, less proactive, would risk underestimating the danger until too late.

BEHIND THE SCENES

The secret of Saddam Hussein's world influence was his skill at lying: specifically, his ability to conceal whether he had weapons of mass destruction.

A credible threat is always more powerful than its execution because it inspires fear without compelling action in response. After 9/11, uncertainty itself became a powerful weapon damaging world travel, trade, and quality of life. Unwilling to accept no-answer-at-all indefinitely, the United States, Britain, and a few determined allies called Saddam Hussein's bluff. Today, thanks to this widely unpopular but effective action, Saddam Hussein's power to frighten us with lies has ended.

The U.S.-led campaigns in Afghanistan and Iraq have achieved other important objectives. Both these nations are no longer potential arsenals and training grounds for attacks on the United States and others but testing grounds for democratic government in a non-Western cultural context. Both are evolving from places where rule by terror was the norm into places where terrorist acts are sporadic, local distractions. Instead of dictating orders affecting every citizen at all times, those who practice terror in Iraq and Afghanistan today are now "outsiders"—still dangerous, still able to kill and maim but no longer operating unopposed. They have been demoted from "rulers" to "spoilers."

While daily TV scenes of attacks and casualties are grim and saddening, we need to recognize these incidents for what they really are: street theater. The blood and wreckage look impressive, but the long-term damage to society is small. Compare the crime dramas many of us also watch on TV. Every show new crimes occur and new criminals appear; but does this repetition make the cops quit and go home? Does a string of unsolved crimes make friends and families of the victims more inclined to join the criminals?

Like Saddam Hussein's lies, the blood-and-fire shows put on by terrorists for world TV succeed only if the audience they play to allows fear to dominate reason. If observers dare to question what they see and peek behind the curtain, they can find the truth and stop being afraid.

WHERE DO WE GO FROM HERE?

The United States and its allies can take pride in their successes against terrorists. Yet no one claims terrorism has been wholly defeated in Afghanistan or Iraq, let alone worldwide. Terrorists' power to occupy and safely hold territory has been greatly reduced, but they still kill people and destroy property. Can they ever be stopped?

The threat from individuals acting alone may never be entirely eliminated. The power of modern weapons and the ease with which they can be obtained has made murderous attacks by disgruntled employees, jealous spouses, or alienated loners familiar incidents around the world. In the future, we will likely need to guard against lone terrorists as we already guard against muggers, thieves, and vandals. Those crimes are universally condemned. Someday, terrorism, too, will be despised as simply crimes of violence directed not against individuals but whole populations.

"The War on Terror" is ultimately a campaign to rally world opinion against the use of indiscriminate killing and destruction to make people afraid. How much money, years of work, and, sadly, human lives must be lost to achieve this global change of heart is still impossible to calculate, but the cost will certainly be high.

The justification for such enormous effort and expense is that so long as terrorism perpetrated by organized groups is tolerated anywhere, no nation can reliably protect its highly vulnerable physical infrastructure or the communication networks that sustain and increasingly interlink global society.[3]

SECURING THE FUTURE

To even attempt such an effort presupposes the belief that it is possible to shape a better future through human will and planning. This belief is especially strong in the United States.

Through most of history, what an individual living in Europe, Africa, or Asia could expect from life was largely predetermined by social position, family ties, and local custom. Such restraints have had less force in the United States. From the start, this has been a land of the future—where heritage and reputation generally mattered less than daring, ability to improvise, and a knack for learning from experience.

Cruelty and injustice have also been part of America's growth. Slavery and exploitation, violence against nature, and countless instances of greed and theft on a grand scale all splash shameful stains across the picture we would like to paint of the United States as a land of freedom and opportunity for all.[4]

However, admitting our failures does not mean those failures outweigh our successes. The history of the United States shows freedom and opportunity being extended more widely and more fairly throughout the population with each generation. Much still remains to be accomplished, but Americans know that progress IS possible because so much progress has already been made.

WORDS AND ACTIONS

One element that has helped the United States to build through generations toward a still unrealized ideal is our written constitution. This document established a form of government and system of laws that recognize the will of the majority as rightly powerful, while at the same time safeguarding the interests of minorities, and offering ways for individuals and groups to disagree, yet coexist within a viable society.

This is the gift and burden we are offering Iraq—a constitution: one that will empower and protect their citizens to dream of a future and then work to build it. In broad outline, the final document will likely reflect our own two-centuries-long experience. But the Iraqis themselves must work out its details.

This achievement will be just one small step toward ending the global threat of terrorism. But for Iraq, a nation long torn by factional fighting, old resentments, and deep mutual mistrust, a truly democratic constitution will make a giant stride toward a sustainable future.

Before we decide that the cost of maintaining a front-line defense against terrorism in Iraq is too high, consider the long-term costs of allowing terrorism to triumph anywhere unchallenged.

It took years of wrangling and debate for delegates to draft the U.S. Constitution. After just a few months, it seems far too soon to abandon hope for a workable constitution in Iraq despite the obvious divisions, frustrations, threats, quarrels, and armed violence in the streets. The whole world has a stake in Iraq's success.

FOOTNOTES

1   How people act often depends more on what they believe is possible than what they know to be true. Great storytellers from Homer to Hemingway, Scheherazade to Dorothy Parker, remain popular long after the worlds they lived in have vanished or greatly changed because their characters stand the test of time. For this reason, insights from fiction and poetry sometimes shed light on real life more effectively than "expert" assessments based on biased or imperfect data. As you read this essay, try to think of stories, poems, or shows you know that offer parallels to post-9/11 events in Iraq and elsewhere. For an example of how this can be done, check out the Web site of the Goethe Institut (a German cultural center) in Washington D.C., which features a number of German poems with English translations, all selected by readers to help us understand complex issues facing the world today. The Internet address for this site is: <http://www.goethe.de/uk/was/lyrik>.

2   It is worth noting that acts of terrorism in the United States have come from many sources and all have been treated as crimes, not political statements or military attacks. See *Target USA: The Inside Story of the New Terrorist War*, by Louis R. Mizell, Jr. (1998), which

reviews dozens of incidents since 1980. For a gripping and revealing look at pre-9/11 U.S. attitudes and expectations regarding global terrorism, read John D. MacDonald's Travis McGee thriller, *The Green Ripper* (1979).

3   How much is really too much to pay? There may be valid reasons for a nation to abandon a long hard job partway through. In a democracy, it is ultimately the voters, not government officials, who make this decision. But giving up simply to save expense is a sad comment on a society's priorities and values. Writing in 1969, British poet Philip Larkin expressed the shame he felt after hearing economic arguments for global retreat in these lines: "Next year we shall be living in a country/That brought its soldiers home for lack of money./...Our children will not know it's a different country./All we can hope to leave them now is money." See "Homage to a Government" in Philip Larkin, *Collected Poems* (UK: 1988; U.S.: 1989).

4   Poverty and injustice exist in the United States as elsewhere. But few Americans remain content to passively accept their "lot in life." Overcoming poverty and oppression is a major theme in popular American writing, from Horatio Alger's *Ragged Dick* (1867), to F. Scott Fitzgerald's *The Great Gatsby* (1925), to Alice Walker's *The Color Purple* (1982). Whether success also brings happiness is another matter and depends on character more than situation. All our Constitution promises is the opportunity for "the pursuit of happiness." Still, this is more than many countries can offer, and it may be fairly claimed that this particular dream is America's most successful export.

Epilogue

Three things cannot long be hidden: the sun, the moon, and the truth.
—Colin L. Powell, U.S. Secretary of State

Writing on December 15, 2003, I expect our attention over the months ahead will probably go to such strategic questions as:

1) How can we improve safeguards against terrorist acts here and abroad—while honoring our civil liberties?
2) How can we improve our intelligence-gathering system—while safeguarding our American Way of Life?
3) How can we mend fences with peeved allies—while steering our own course?
4) How can we help lead the UN and NATO—while steering our own course?
5) How can we manage the costs of helping the governments of both Afghanistan and Iraq—while helping the many in need in our own country?
6) How can we increase our military head count and boost quality—while avoiding restarting the Draft?
7) How can we assure no backsliding in Iraq—while respecting the autonomy of a new Iraqi government?
8) How can we successfully try Saddam Hussein—even while he looks "forward to the mother of all genocide trials [and intends] to pose as the great Arab hero...." (Safire).
9) How can we persuade the Iraqis to allow the Hussein trial to be run under UN auspices by international and Iraqi judges (Anon., Editorial)?
10) How can we convince the so-called "dead-enders," the die-hard Hussein backers to lay down their arms—as perhaps by granting a full amnesty for the foot soldiers of both the Baath regime and the insurgency?

11) How can we speed a high-quality rebuilding of the country—while safeguarding against profiteering and corruption?

12) How can we help Iraq create "a new vision for itself—in fact, a whole new cultural and political identity to replace the old Arab nationalist ideal?" (Marr)

These, and other vexing challenges that will develop along the way, should find coverage in our next volume of original essays. Attention will go not only to "what" we do, but also to "how" we do it.

In sum, it would seem in fall 2003 we had finally begun to come to grips with all that the War on Terrorism entailed. As *New York Times* columnist Tom Friedman advised, we were beginning to understand we must not overreact. We must tread softly and care deeply. We must find communities of shared values, secure our alliances, and deter terrorists by not being terrorized. We must tackle the 12 challenges above, and remember to also protect time and energy to enjoy life ("Terrorists win when they prevent us from enjoying and spreading our values.") (Friedman). Difficult? Absolutely! Doable? We have to find out.

REFERENCES

Editorial, "The Capture of a Dictator." *New York Times*, 15 December 2003. A-26.

Friedman, Thomas L. "The Way We Were." *New York Times*, 23 November 2003. WK-11.

Marr, Phebe. "Saddam's Past, Iraq's Future." *New York Times*, 15 December 2003. A-27.

Safire, William. "From the 'Spider Hole.'" *New York Times*, 15 December 2003. A-27.

ABSTRACTS from *FUTURE SURVEY* (*FS*)

The following abstracts were first published in *Future Survey*, a nonpartisan monthly publication of the World Future Society in Bethesda, Maryland. Written by its originator and editor, Michael Marien, *FS* provides 50 abstracts every month of recent books, reports, and important articles on both global and domestic issues. In addition to items directly relevant to the Iraq War, *FS* carries items on related topics such as world futures, the global economy, the Middle East, development issues, security and disarmament, energy alternatives, and the global environment.

From *Future Survey*, October 2003

SECURITY—SECURITY/FOREIGN POLICY 25:10/475 (A)

The Illusion of Control: Force and Foreign Policy in the Twenty-First Century. Seyom Brown (Professor of International Cooperation, Brandeis University). Washington: Brookings Institution Press, May 2003, 196p.

An analysis of the growing willingness of U.S. government officials to use force, implications for the U.S., and guidelines for avoiding consequences adverse to basic U.S. interests.

Contemporary pressures for "muscular diplomacy" and "preemptive war" stem from three fundamental developments: 1) transition from the relatively orderly superpower-dominated world of the last half century to a disorderly and increasingly "polyarchic" world in which U.S. hegemony is challenged by numerous actors; 2) the increasing disposition of U.S. officials to threaten use of force to keep the most dangerous aspects of the emerging polyarchy under control; 3) the promise of the so-called revolution in military affairs to bring an unprecedented degree of controllability to the conduct of war (as new technology promises to keep casualties very low, champions of RMA say that "Bound to Lead" need not mean "bound to bleed"). However, a foreign policy animated by optimistic estimates of the efficacy of force is likely to pull the U.S. into excessive commitments and imprudent action. "It is an illusion to believe that war's inherently limited controllability can somehow be fundamentally transformed through technological innovation." War, even high-tech war, should still be held in awe as the beast it has always been, capable of sometimes destroying those who try to control it.

Some guidelines for using military power: 1) the overarching guideline is to keep the threshold between nonviolent diplomacy and war thick and clear; 2) be assured that the interests and values at stake are of sufficient weight to warrant going to war; 3) be convinced that resorting to military force will better serve the interests at stake than will nonmilitary actions, and that likely harm will not exceed the expected good; 4) be willing to commit to whatever postwar responsibilities and resources will be needed to restore at least minimal civic life where it has been severely disrupted ("there should be no illusions that the required international cooperation will always be forthcoming, especially in cases in which U.S. military operations have been essentially unilateral"); 5) explicitly define and reinforce "firebreaks" between different kinds and levels of warfare.

SECURITY/TECHNOLOGY   25:10/468 (AB)

Limiting the Tools of War (five articles). *Issues in Science and Technology*, 19:3, Spring 2003, 47–78.

1) "Controlling Dangerous Pathogens," by John D. Steinbruner and Elisa D. Harris (both Center for International and Security Studies, University of Maryland) argues that remarkable advances are underway in the biological sciences, but more systemic protection is needed to guard against deliberate or inadvertent creation of advanced disease agents: "the ability to alter basic life processes is not matched by a corresponding

ability to understand or manage the potentially negative consequences of such research."

2) "Cybersecurity: Who's Watching the Store?" by Bruce
Berkowitz (Hoover Institution) and Robert W. Hahn (AEI)
warn that most government agencies have yet to take effective
action to make infosystems more secure, and we are still flying
blind in a public policy sense [see *FS 25:5/224* for full abstract].

3) "The Case Against New Nuclear Weapons" by Michael
A. Levi (Strategic Security Project, Federation of American
Scientists) worries about the misguided effort to develop a new
weapons system called the "robust nuclear earth penetrator"
(RNEP); advocates of new tactical nuclear weapons tend to
focus only on simple destructive power.

4) "Time to Sign the Mine Ban Treaty" by Richard A.
Matthew and Ted Gaulin (Global Environmental Change and
Human Security Project, UC-Irvine) question the refusal of the
U.S. to sign the MBT because of claims that antipersonnel land-
mines are vital to the security of U.S. soldiers in Korea.

5) "'Nonlethal' Chemical Weapons: A Faustian Bargain" by
Mark Wheelis (UC-Davis) warns that incapacitants developed
for use by law enforcement are more likely to be used by terrorists, dictators, or criminals; "use of chemical incapacitants is
likely to be the first step in the exploitation of pharmacology
and biotechnology for hostile purposes."

[NOTE: Despite absence of the "technology assessment" phrase, all
of these authors are engaged in a sort of TA, and all of these essays
strongly imply that a visible, independent, and well-funded Office of
Technology Assessment is badly needed somewhere in U.S. society.]

SECURITY/TERRORISM   25:10/474 (AB)

The Protean Enemy. Jessica Stern (Lecturer in Public Policy, Harvard University), *Foreign Affairs*, 82:4, July-August 2003, 27–40.

Author of *The Ultimate Terrorists* on WMD terrorist threats
(Harvard UP, 1999; *FS 21:5/235*) argues that the modern
exemplar of Proteus (a Greek sea god assuming many faces) is

al Qaeda and its affiliates, which remain "among the most significant threats to U.S. national security today." Having suffered the destruction of its sanctuary in Afghanistan, al Qaeda's already decentralized organization has become more decentralized still.

Yet despite setbacks, intelligence officials in the U.S., Europe, and Africa report that "al Qaeda has stepped up its recruitment drive in response to the war in Iraq." The target audience for recruitment has changed: more are converts to Islam, more are women, more are younger and with an even more "menacing attitude" according to a French official. The organization's "remarkably protean nature" accounts for its ongoing effectiveness in the face of an unprecedented onslaught: it has constantly evolved and shown a surprising willingness to adapt its mission to attract new recruits and allies and to make it harder to detect and destroy.

The willingness to forge unlikely alliances is shown by the growing evidence that al Qaeda, a Sunni organization, is now cooperating with the Shi'a group Hezbollah, considered to be the most sophisticated terrorist group in the world.

Mixing and matching of capabilities, swapping of training, and use of common facilities has become the hallmark of professional terrorists today. The Internet has greatly facilitated the spread of virtual subcultures, and has "substantially increased the capacity of loosely networked terrorist organizations." Terrorists have also started to forge ties with traditional organized crime groups, especially in India. Another set of unlikely links has sprung up in U.S. prisons, where Saudi charities now fund organizations that preach radical Islam.

"Totalitarian Islamist revivalism has become the ideology of the dystopian new world order. In an earlier era, radicals might have described their grievances through other ideological lenses, perhaps anarchism, Marxism, or Nazism. Today they choose extreme Islamism." Radical transnational Islam, divorced from its countries of origin, appeals to some jobless youths in depressed parts of Europe and the U.S. Some white supremacists and extremist Christians applaud al Qaeda's rejectionist goals and may eventually contribute to al Qaeda missions.

Correct U.S. policies could do much to diminish the appeal of rejectionist groups, e.g., better funding for secular education in countries such as Pakistan and correcting the chaos in Afghanistan and postwar Iraq. To prevent terrorists from acquiring new weapons, Western governments must make it harder for radicals to get their hands on them. In sum, the U.S. must match the radical innovation shown by al Qaeda and other terrorists, and show a willingness to adopt new methods and new ways of thinking.

SECURITY/TECHNOLOGY   25:10/467 (B)

"The Second Nuclear Age" (Cover Feature), Bill Keller, *New York Times Magazine*, 4 May 2003, 48–53 ff.

The first nuclear age began over Hiroshima, eventually maturing into a great standoff between the U.S. and the Soviet Union. Despite a number of nuclear near misses in the first 20 years, the two rivals slowly brought their fearsome weapons under control and negotiated a protocol for living with them. During the same period, other potential nuclear states were restrained by treaties, the threat of sanctions and other diplomatic pressures, and by the superpowers' semi-monopoly on technology.

The second nuclear age began when India detonated five test blasts in 1998, with Pakistan reciprocating two weeks later. Both countries were known to be developing nuclear weapons, but they came out of the closet brazenly. These were nuclear weapons with a regional agenda, unveiled with a populist flourish and with a religious subtext. By many estimates, India and Pakistan are forerunners of a new kind of nuclear power.

The first nuclear era was primarily a boxer's clinch of two great industrial powers, each claiming to represent an ideology of global appeal. The new era is about insecure nations, most of them led by autocrats and the relatively poor, residing in rough neighborhoods, unaligned with and resentful of Western power. North Korea is seen as already nuclear. Iran is believed to be moving rapidly toward acquiring nukes. Libya and Syria are watched with suspicion. Experts talk of a nuclear Iran inspiring nuclear lust in Egypt, Turkey, even Saudi Arabia, and of a nuclear North Korea prompting a breakout in Japan, South Korea, even Taiwan.

The arsenals of the first nuclear age were governed by elaborate rules and sophisticated technology designed to prevent firing in haste. Some of the newcomers are thought to have far less rigorous command and control, raising fears that lines of authority could be abandoned in the heat of battle. Moreover, there is the danger of third-world weapons or weapons-grade material falling into the hands of terrorists. In the first nuclear age, the secrets and ingredients of bomb-making were closely held. In the second nuclear age, globalization seems to have made nuclear weaponry just another unsavory but probably uncontainable technology, like Internet porn.

The world of people who worry about nuclear weapons is now divided into two hostile camps. The traditional arms controllers advocate treaties, export controls, international agencies and sanctions. The "new and ascendant camp" of "counter-proliferationists," including the Bush regime, argues that the old constraints have broken down and show a greater willingness to use force to pre-empt a threat. Arms controllers see this group as unilateralists, carelessly provocative in their speech and quick to reach for a gun. In turn, counter-proliferators paint traditional arms controllers as idealists and wishful thinkers.

SECURITY/TECHNOLOGY/TERRORISM   25:10/466 (BC)
Avoiding Armageddon: Our Future, Our Choice. Martin Schram (Scripps Howard News Service), New York: Basic Books, 2003, 256p.

Companion volume to the PBS Series from Ted Turner Documentaries, with chapters in four parts: 1) Reversing the Nuclear Race: tales of nuclear theft and nuclear security gaps in Russia, nuclear nightmare scenarios (a nuclear reactor for electric power as a de facto dirty bomb for terrorists), a history of nuclear proliferation, South Asia's nuclear crisis, nuclear waste in Russia, the Nunn-Lugar Cooperative Threat Reduction program to secure Russian WMDs (a global partnership is needed), the goal of "de-alerting" strategic forces ("At present, the U.S. and Russia each have about 2,000 nuclear weapons that are kept on hair-trigger alert status; they pack the power of 100,000 Hiroshima-sized bombs");

2) Chemical and Biological Arsenals: the "urgent crisis" of securing and destroying huge arsenals vulnerable to terrorists and the ravages of corrosion (in addition to eight declared stockpiles in the U.S., there are 229 "non-stockpiles" of abandoned toxic chemicals and old chemical munitions in numerous unmarked landfills), Russian stockpiles of bioweapons, bioterror threats in the U.S.;

3) Terrorism: Osama bin Laden and al Qaeda, terrorism through the ages (dating from the Zealots Zachari sect in the first century A.D.), the psychology of suicide bombers;

4) Future Solutions: Toward Feeling Safe Again: securing homelands (a job that can never be done to total satisfaction), nation building in Afghanistan, combating AIDS, the Global Marshall Plan proposal of Britain's Gordon Brown [see *FS* 24:2/060], the UN Millennium Goals to be met by 2015, steep reductions in nuclear weapons.

[NOTE: Covers a wide swath of ground with fact, anecdote, and interviews. Even so, global warming and the many other aspects of "Ecological Security," as detailed by Dennis Pirages (*FS* 25:9/403) are not dealt with here.]

SECURITY/HOMELAND   25:10/472 (AB)

Protecting the American Homeland: One Year On. Michael E. O'Hanlon and seven others (Brookings Foreign Policy Studies program). Washington D.C.: Brookings Institution Press, April 2003, 188p.

An updated version of *Protecting the American Homeland: A Preliminary Analysis* (Brookings, April 2002) with a new 28-page preface added. Since the September 11 attacks, much has been done to protect the safety of Americans. Americans are on the alert (providing a critical first line of defense), air travel is much safer, intelligence sharing has improved, suspicious ships entering U.S. waters are screened more frequently, early steps have been taken to reduce exposure to biological attacks, oversight has been tightened on labs working with biomaterials, and certain types of major infrastructure are now protected when terrorism alerts suggest that such measures are necessary.

"But much, much more remains to be done." Most of the above steps reflect a response to past tactics of al Qaeda, and do not anticipate possible future means by which terrorist groups might try to harm Americans.

The Bush administration's strategy leaves out four key priorities for action that the authors advocated in April 2002 and continue to believe important: 1) Major infrastructure in the private sector, which the Bush administration largely ignores (e.g., the chemical and trucking industries have not moved adequately on their own to improve safety, leaving their assets vulnerable to theft or sabotage);

2) The administration still has no plan for quickly improving real-time information sharing in the national law enforcement community and among the broader set of public and private actors vital to preventing and responding to homeland attacks;

3) The presently unrecognized need to greatly expand certain specific capacities for homeland security such as the Coast Guard and Customs, as well as security for forms of transport such as trains (Customs "still only inspects <5 percent of all cargo entering the U.S., even if it has become savvier about which small percentage to examine");

4) The administration has taken smart initial steps to bring together terrorism databases of various agencies but has not done enough to anticipate possible next actions of terrorists (e.g., the possibility that civilian airliners could be attacked by small man-portable surface-to-air missiles). In sum, "for every important step that has been taken, an equally important one has been neglected."

A Grand Strategy for America. Robert J. Art (Professor of International Relations, Brandeis University). A Century Foundation Book. Ithaca, N.Y.: Cornell University Press, July 2003, 320p.

"This is a big picture book. It concerns the fundamental direction the U.S. should take in its foreign policy and grand strategy." Grand strategy is a broad subject that tells a nation's leaders what goals they should aim for and how best they can use their military power to attain these goals.

Four basic questions are addressed in devising a grand strategy: 1) What are America's interests in the world and what are the threats to these interests? 2) What are the possible grand strategies to protect America's interests from these threats? (The U.S. possesses an unparalleled margin of power over other states, but this margin of power will not last forever: "the U.S. has perhaps a few decades—probably three at the most—before its considerable edge over others begins to wane significantly"; the future is not likely to be as rosy for the U.S. as in the 1990s, and the next few decades "look more ominous") 3) Which of the grand strategies best protects Americans' national interests? 4) What specific political policies and military capabilities are required to support the grand strategy chosen?

Six overarching national interests for the U.S. are postulated ("the first is vital; the second and third are highly important; the last three are important"): 1) Prevent an attack on the American homeland ("the one truly vital interest of the U.S.");

2) Prevent great-power Eurasian wars and, if possible, the intense security competitions that make them more likely (these wars could drag the U.S. in, promote the spread of WMDs, threaten trade, and bring adverse political change);

3) Preserve access to a reasonably priced and secure supply of oil;

4) Preserve an open international economic order to "help promote the growth of wealth";

5) Foster the spread of democracy and respect for human rights abroad, and prevent genocide or mass murder in civil wars (important because "democratic states help to promote peace");

6) Protect the global environment, especially from the adverse effects of global warming and severe climate change.

These six goals "encompass both realpolitik and liberal internationalist goals." The author favors "selective engagement" as the grand strategy that would best protect America's six national interests ... (a strategy that) steers a middle course between not doing enough and attempting too much. Seven other grand strategies are evaluated: dominion, global collective security, regional collective security, cooperative security, containment, isolationism, and offshore balancing. These strategies are seen as infeasible or undesirable.

[NOTE: Not as much a "big picture" exercise as the author imagines. A more apt twenty-first century approach should be to start first with the overall interests of humanity and then to assess how "state-centric" U.S. interests can be supportive or in conflict with these interests. In doing so, a different set of grand strategies could well arise, appropriate to a globalizing age when the definition of "security" is broadening (see RAND report, 25:10/ 469).]

SECURITY/PUBLIC HEALTH   25:10/469 (AB)

The Global Threat of New and Reemerging Infectious Diseases: Reconciling U.S. National Security and Public Health Policy. Jennifer Brower and Peter Chalk (both RAND Science and Technology, Arlington, Va.). Santa Monica, Calif.: RAND, March 2003, 146p.

The U.S. and most of the world today face little danger from direct military assault from an opposing state. This threat has been supplanted with concerns about "gray area" challenges that face the global community. Emerging security threats such as terrorism, drug-trafficking, and environmental degradation differ significantly from traditional state-centric paradigms. "The increasing transnational threat of infectious disease deserves special attention within this context of the evolving definition of security in the post-Cold War era." State-centric models of security are ineffective at coping with issues such as the spread of disease.

"Human security reflects the new challenges facing society in the twenty-first century. In this model, the primary object of security is the individual, not the state." Infectious disease clearly represents a threat to human security. In addition to threatening the health of an individual, the spread of disease can weaken public confidence in government, have an adverse economic impact, catalyze regional instability, and pose a strategic threat through bioweapons. While infectious diseases are widely discussed, few treatises have addressed the security implications of emerging and reemerging illnesses.

This report seeks a "more comprehensive analysis" of disease and security with two case studies: the AIDS crisis in South Africa and U.S. management of the infectious disease threat.

Roughly 25 percent of South Africa's adult population is currently infected with HIV. "The true impact of the AIDS epidemic is yet to be felt." The number of HIV infections is still increasing, and deaths from full-blown AIDS are not projected to peak until the 2009–2012 period. "The disease is responsible for undermining social and economic stability, weakening military preparedness, contributing to increases in crime and lack of capability to respond to it, and weakening regional stability. Specific effects include creating >2 million orphans and removing some U.S. $22 billion from South Africa's economy.

This case is "a stark reminder of the pervasive and insidious impact that infectious organisms can have on a state's wider stability and viability … the South African case underscores, in the most visible terms, the need for national and international disease preparedness."

The U.S. is currently managing the infectious disease threat, but "there are many indications that, if left unchecked, pathogens could present a serious threat to the smooth functioning of the country." In the last half century, almost 30 new human diseases were identified, and antibiotic and drug resistance grew at an alarming rate. This trend applies equally to animal diseases [e.g., see *FS* 25:9/417 on chronic wasting disease].

"As Americans' exposure to emerging and reemerging pathogens has grown, the country's ability to respond to infectious disease has diminished in many areas." This was recognized in 1992 by the Institute of Medicine, which challenged the nation to respond. But governments at all levels largely failed to do so until the terrorist strikes of September 11, 2001.

Specific actions are proposed to address these shortcomings: enhanced coordination between public health authorities at all levels, integrating the private sector into overall public health efforts, a large-scale education and information campaign, augmenting the supply of healthcare workers, developing appropriate emergency plans, and more resources invested to help foreign governments in disease prevention efforts. Beyond these initiatives, "the U.S. also needs to revisit how it defines security and formulates mechanisms for its provision."

[NOTE: An important bridge to wider appreciation of "ecological security." (*FS* 25:9/453)]

SECURITY/TERRORISM   25:10/471 (A)
Terrorism, Freedom, and Security: Winning Without War. Philip B. Heymann (Professor of Law, Harvard University). Cambridge Mass.: MIT Press, October 2003, 210p.

Author of *Terrorism and America: A Commonsense Strategy for a Democratic Society* (MIT Press, 1998; *FS* 20:10/489) notes that much has changed since his 1998 book, but some things have not changed. Three requirements remain constant about our response to the new, far greater threats of terrorism after September 11: 1) we have to think hard about what we know, and can learn, and what may be effective; 2) we have to recognize that in doing so, unlike in real war, what helps in one way is likely to be damaging in another (e.g., assassinating a terrorist leader may weaken management but help recruitment by creating a martyr); 3) "we cannot ignore the costs to democracy of steps taken in a prolonged effort to deal with a form of attack that will continue to be available to small numbers of angry people for decades."

Topics include terrorism after September 11, the Bush strategy of proclaiming "war on terrorism" (however well it may work in the short term, "it has great weaknesses as a long-term strategy"), the status of the term "war" (it is without real definition in either the law of the U.S. or the law of nations; in the last half-century, declarations of war have become obsolete), the necessity for our strategy to reflect the complexity and uncertainty of the threat, the dangers of relying on the wrong resources (i.e., military force), protection against unidentified terrorists, the importance of intelligence, the impact on democratic freedoms of the Bush administration's questionable domestic strategy of counter-terrorism, the conditions for continuing world leadership (moral leadership requires us to be a model of democracy at home, even under threat), and the problem of drifting into an "Intelligence State" (a scenario of the U.S. in 2010 describes greater efforts to track the movements and activities of all Americans, encouraging citizens to report remote suspicions about their neighbors, the routine use of torturers and murderers to further U.S. intelligence and safety, etc.).

In sum, "for security against terrorism we need, most of all, cooperative international intelligence and law enforcement activities, not bold attacks by a powerful military." The dangers from well-armed terrorists will outlast any single embodiment such as al Qaeda; so must our democratic traditions.

[NOTE: A thoughtful critique of the U.S. "war" on terrorism.]

SECURITY/TERRORISM   25:10/473 (B)

Understanding Terrorism: Challenges, Perspectives, and Issues. Gus Martin (Cal State University-Dominguez Hills). Thousand Oaks, Calif.: Sage Publications, 2003, 413p.

Textbook with chapters in four parts: 1) Conceptual Review: historical perspectives, definitions, ideologies, the morality of terrorist violence, extremism as the foundation of terrorism, "the new terrorism" (aiming not at political demands but at the destruction of society), motives of terrorists (simplified views of good and evil, codes of self-sacrifice, seeking utopias, acts of political will); 2) The Terrorists: terror from above (state terrorism as foreign and domestic policy), terror from below (dissident terrorism, ethno-nationalist terrorism), terrorism on the left and right, religious terrorism, criminal terrorism, international terrorist networks; 3) The Terrorist Trade: typical objectives, terrorist methods and targets, the role of the media in publicizing the cause; 4) Terrorism in the U.S.: left- and right-wing terrorism, options (repression, conciliation, legalistic responses).

Final chapter covers The Future of Terrorism: 1) the sources of extremist behavior in the modern era will remain unchanged in the near future; people who have been relegated to the social and political margins will form factions that resort to violence; 2) terrorism in various regions will continue (ethno-national communal conflict in Africa, political violence in some Asian nations, international terrorists using Europe as a battleground; Latin American terrorism likely to be sporadic but on a lower scale of intensity than in the past); 3) many good reasons to presume that new technologies will be acquired and used, especially combined with the motivations and morality of the New Terrorism; 4) the near future of international terrorism in the U.S. will be quite threatening.

[NOTE: Very "textbooky," with boxes, charts of key terms, further readings, and argument outlines. Nevertheless, the scope may be valuable. ALSO SEE another textbook: *Terrorism in Perspective* by Pamala L. Griset and Sue Mahan, both University of Central Florida (Sage, 2003/391p), with chapters on the history of terrorism, international terrorism, domestic terrorism in the U.S., the media and terrorism, terrorist tactics, and counterterrorism—much like the Martin text. The main distinction is a chapter on "Women as Terrorists."]

SECURITY/DEFENSE POLICY   25:10/477 (AB)

Reshaping America's Military: Four Alternatives Presented as Presidential Speeches. Laurence J. Korb (VP, CFR). A Council Policy Initiative. New York: Council on Foreign Relations, December 2002, 96p.

This report is fashioned as a Memorandum to the U.S. President, making the best cases for four plausible defense policies, articulated as four speeches that each present a clear strategic thrust. The four options: 1) Enhanced Defense: the U.S. is the sole superpower and must substantially increase spending to match our expansive interests and the unique burden of superpower status; we must upgrade military superiority almost across the board, increasing the share of GDP spent on defense from 3 percent to 4 percent ("this course is favored by the Secretary of Defense, the Joint Chiefs of Staff, and many conservatives in both parties");

2) Revolutionary Transformation: we must immediately begin making heavy investments in revolutionary technologies to insure that we can defeat potential future adversaries; we must provide our forces with information superiority, safety through stealth, superior striking speed, agility, and mobility; we should also deploy missile defenses and make significant cuts in our nuclear arsenal ("this option is supported by many defense experts in Congress as well as defense intellectuals");

3) Evolutionary Transformation: the U.S. faces serious threats to its security and we must rebuild existing capability to combat them while continuing to invest in future technology ("this course is favored by a majority of the Democrats in Congress and by most of our allies");

4) Cooperative Defense: the war against terrorism clearly shows that the U.S. cannot and should not attempt to meet the array of existing threats by itself; instead, we should cooperate with our allies and help build international institutions to share the necessary security responsibilities; a benefit of this approach is that we can eventually reduce military spending by 15–20 percent by ridding ourselves of a wasteful military still

shaped too much by Cold War thinking and investing in antiterrorism agencies such as the Coast Guard, FBI, CIA, and INS ("this option is supported by traditional internationalists in Congress and the arms-control community"). Pros and cons of each option are discussed, as well as the political impact.

SECURITY/DEFENSE POLICY   25:10/478 (AB)
Corporate Warriors: The Rise of the Privatized Military Industry. P.W. Singer (Olin Fellow, Foreign Policy Studies Program, Brookings Institution). Ithaca, N.Y.: Cornell University Press, July 2003, 330p.

The monopoly of the state over violence is the exception in world history, not the rule. Ancient history is replete with stories of hired, foreign troops, e.g., it was a general practice for ancient Greek armies to build up their forces by hiring outside specialists. Through the centuries, private military organizations particularly thrived in periods of systemic transition, when governments were weakened and powerful military capacity was available on the open market.

Since states started to replace rule by kings and princes in the 1600s, military services have been kept within the political realm under the control of the public sector. This public monopoly of the military profession is now breaking up. A new global industry of Privatized Military Firms (PMFs) has emerged, involving business organizations that trade in professional services linked to warfare. "The end of the Cold War is at the heart of the emergence of the privatized military industry." It removed controls over the levels of conflict, while also releasing unresolved tensions.

When the Cold War ended, the labor market was flooded with soldiers from downsized militaries especially in the Communist Bloc but also in the U.S. (which has one-third fewer soldiers than at its Cold War peak). Not only was there a glut of trained military personnel but also the tools for large-scale violence. Massive arms stocks have become available to the open market at cut-rate prices (e.g., nearly every weapon in the East German arsenal was sold, most of it to private bidders).

Two other long-term trends were necessary to the emergence of the industry: the broad transformations in the nature of warfare itself (creating new market opportunities for PMFs) and the privatization revolution, which provided the logic, legitimacy, and models.

A tour around the world suggests the full extent and activity of PMFs. In Africa, "PMFs are almost pervasive" (>80 firms offer military services of some sort in Angola). In Europe, the commander of the Kosovo Liberation Army received training from MPRI (see below). The British military exemplifies the trend to military outsourcing and a recent initiative authorizes the entire transfer of key military services (e.g., the army's tank transporter unit) to private companies. Military firm activity is quite significant in the Middle East, with several prominent firms based in Israel. PMFs have been active in many Asian states (several French firms are rumored to have helped train the local military in Burma). In the Americas, at least seven U.S.-based military companies are active in Colombia. In Mexico, several corporations, including the Jose Cuervo distillery, have hired their own private armies. From 1994–2002, the U.S. Defense Department entered into more than 3,000 contracts with U.S.-based firms, with an estimated value of >$300 billion.

"There is no doubt that provision of military services is a growing industry." Best estimates are of annual market revenue in the range of $100 billion; "by 2010, the industry is expected to at least double in revenue." The true boom lies shortly ahead because the market is far from saturated. "Few dampening forces loom, while pressures for further expansion remain on the rise."

Separate chapters are devoted to profiling exemplars of three types of firms: 1) The Military Provider: Pretoria-based Executive Outcomes, founded in 1989 by the elite forces of the apartheid-era South African Defence Force, is perhaps the best known; although it dissolved itself in 1999, it was the most notorious example of a military provider in its purest form;

2) The Military Consulting Firm: Military Professional Resource Inc. (MPRI), drawn from the highest levels of retired U.S. military personnel, is one of the best-known players (a key asset is a carefully managed database of >12,500 on-call former military personnel, roughly 95 percent from the U.S. Army (the firm helped Croatia train its military, provides various training services to the U.S. military, and now manages ROTC programs in >200 universities);

3) The Military Support Firm: one of the dominant companies in the field is Brown & Root Services (BRS; also known as Kellogg, Brown & Root, or KBR), a division of Halliburton Co. (headed by now-Vice President Dick Cheney from 1995–2000), which is now the fifth-largest military contractor.

At their best, PMFs may equal public institutions in protecting society; but "their market lacks any measure of regulation and has certain propensities for moral harms." The new PMF industry "poses issues and challenges that must be addressed by governments, militaries, humanitarian advocates, and beyond."

A pressing policy concern is the lazy and haphazard way in which governments have privatized their military services over the last decade: the fact that one can outsource does not always mean one should. Regulating this industry like any other industry is an important concern. Supplanting the old proverb that "War is far too important to be left to the generals," a new adage for the twenty-first century may be necessary: "War is far too important to be left to private industry."

[NOTE: Fascinating and essential. This powerful argument would be still stronger if the privatization of domestic security services were also mentioned as a parallel trend. Includes a list of 61 PMFs and their Web sites. ALSO SEE "Outsourcing War: An Inside Look at Brown & Root, the Kingpin of America's New Military-Industrial Complex," *Business Week* Special Report, 15 September 2003, 69–78.]

SECURITY/METHODS   25:10/470 (ABC)

Beyond Fear: Thinking Sensibly About Security in an Uncertain World. Bruce Schneier (www.schneier.com; Founder and CTO, Counterpane Internet Security). New York: Copernicus Books, September 2003, 295p.

A "professional thinker about security" and author of *Applied Cryptography* (1994), said to have sold >200,000 copies, applies the methods developed for computer security to broader security issues, especially security against terrorism. "Security issues affect us more and more in our daily lives, and we should all make an effort to understand them better. We need to stop accepting uncritically what politicians and pundits are telling us. We need to move beyond fear and start making sensible security trade-offs."

Everyone makes security trade-offs, every day. We live our lives making judgments, assessments, assumptions, and choices about security (e.g., when we lock the door to our home, we make a security trade-off: the inconvenience of using a key in exchange for some security against burglary).

Making security trade-offs isn't some mystical art: "the goal of this book is to demystify security, to help you move beyond fear." To get beyond fear, you have to start thinking intelligently about trade-offs, the risks you face, and the options for dealing with those risks. A lot of lousy security is available for purchase, and a lot of lousy security is imposed on us by government. Once we move beyond fear, we can recognize bad or overpriced security.

No security is foolproof but neither is all security equal. There's cheap security and expensive security, unobtrusive security and security that forces change in how we live. There's security that respects our liberties and security that doesn't. "A common path to bad security is knee-jerk reactions to the news of the day. Too much of the U.S. government's response post-9/11 is exactly that." Most of the changes we're being asked to endure won't result in good security. They're Band-Aids® that ignore the real problems.

"Security is always a trade-off, and to ignore or deny those trade-offs is to risk losing basic freedoms and ways of life we now take for granted." Security exists to deal with a few bad apples. It's a tax on the honest. Perfect security is impractical because the costs are simply too high. And despite a plethora of security systems in every aspect of our lives, "none of these systems is perfect." The challenge is to figure out what to keep, what to alter, what to toss, and what to build from scratch. The status quo is never done, because security is never done. It has no beginning and no ending. "Words like 'always' and 'never,' when used to describe security solutions, are major contributors to bad security decisions."

A five-step process is used to analyze and evaluate security systems, technologies, and practices: 1) What assets are you trying to protect? 2) What are the risks to these assets? 3) How well does the security solution mitigate those risks? 4) What other risks does the security solution cause (in that most solutions cause new problems)? 5) What costs and trade-offs does the security solution impose?

[NOTE: Simply written, with wisdom for everyone, at every level—from personal and family security to organization and nation. Schneier's ideas were profiled in "Homeland Insecurity" by Charles C. Mann (*The Atlantic Monthly*, September 2002, 82–102).]

Results in Iraq:
100 Days toward Security and Freedom

August 8, 2003, marked the hundredth day since the end of major combat operations in Iraq. Results in Iraq: 100 Days Toward Security and Freedom presents highlights of the successes shared by post-Saddam Iraqis and their partners in the renewal of their nation.

Under the leadership of the Coalition Provisional Authority (CPA) and the new Iraqi Governing Council, major strides are being planned and made in three key areas: security, economic stability and growth, and democracy. As this report is issued, the CPA is working with Iraqis to implement a strategic plan with measurable goals.

Outside observers and coalition leaders agree that much remains to be done to restore order and bring prosperity to a brutalized society and an infrastructure suffering from decades of malign neglect. The steps toward sovereignty and democracy will be difficult and require patience and time. Substantial progress is being made on all fronts.

As President Bush said last week, the "success of a free Iraq will ... demonstrate to other countries in that region that national prosperity and dignity are found in representative government and free institutions.... As freedom advances in the Middle East, those societies will be less likely to produce ideologies of hatred and produce recruits for terror."

This report focuses on 10 areas where the liberation of Iraq has improved the lives of Iraqis and the safety and security of the world. Some examples in this report include:

1. For the first time in the lives of most Iraqis, a representative government is being established and human rights and freedom are being enshrined.
2. Nearly three dozen countries are contributing financially to the renewal of Iraq, and 19 countries are providing personnel for Operation Iraqi Freedom.

3. The food distribution system is functioning, based on equitable needs rather than cronyism.
4. Nearly all Iraqi children have finished exams from last year. All universities are open.
5. A $53 million program to rehabilitate more than 100 schools and clinics is underway.

10 Ways the Liberation of Iraq Supports the War on Terror

1. With the fall of Saddam Hussein's regime, Iraq is no longer a state sponsor of terror. According to State Department reports on terrorism, before the removal of Saddam's regime, Iraq was one of seven state sponsors of terror.
2. Saddam Hussein's regime posed a threat to the security of the United States and the world. With the removal of Saddam Hussein's regime, a leader who pursued, used, and possessed weapons of mass destruction is no longer in power.
3. Saddam Hussein would not uphold his international commitments, and now that he is no longer in power, the world is safe from this tyrant. The old Iraqi regime defied the international community and seventeen UN resolutions for twelve years and gave every indication that it would never disarm and never comply with the just demands of the world.
4. A senior al Qaida terrorist, now detained, who had been responsible for al Qaida training camps in Afghanistan, reports that al Qaida was intent on obtaining WMD assistance from Iraq. According to a credible, high-level al Qaida source, Usama Bin Laden and deceased al Qaida leader Muhammad Atif did not believe that al Qaida labs in Afghanistan were capable of manufacturing chemical and biological weapons, so they turned to Iraq for assistance. Iraq agreed to provide chemical and biological weapons training for two al Qaida associates starting in December 2000.

5. Senior al Qaida associate Abu Musab al-Zarqawi came to Baghdad in May 2002 for medical treatment along with approximately two dozen al Qaida terrorist associates. This group stayed in Baghdad and other parts of Iraq and plotted terrorist attacks around the world.

6. A safe haven in Iraq belonging to Ansar al-Islam—a terrorist group closely associated with Zarqawi and al Qaida—was destroyed during Operation Iraqi Freedom. In March 2003, during a raid on the compound controlled by the terrorists in northeastern Iraq, a cache of documents was discovered, including computer discs and foreign passports belonging to fighters from various Middle East nationalities.

7. The al Qaida affiliate Ansar al-Islam is known to still be present in Iraq. Such terrorist groups are now plotting against U.S. forces in Iraq.

8. Law enforcement and intelligence operations have disrupted al Qaida associate Abu Musab al-Zarqawi's poison plotting in France, Britain, Spain, Italy, Germany, and Russia. The facilities in northern Iraq, set up by Zarqawi and Ansar al-Islam were, before the war, an al Qaida's poisons/toxins laboratory.

9. Abu Musab al-Zarqawi, the al Qaida associate with direct links to Iraq, oversaw those responsible for the assassination of USAID officer Laurence Foley in Amman, Jordan, last October.

10. Saddam Hussein's Iraq provided material assistance to Palestinian terrorist groups, including the Popular Front for the Liberation of Palestine-General Command, HAMAS, and the Palestine Islamic Jihad, according to a State Department report. This included paying the families of Palestinian suicide bombers, according to testimonials from Palestinians and cancelled checks. Also, according to State Department reports, terrorist groups the Iranian Mujahedin-e-Khalq and the Abu Nidal organization were protected by the Iraqi regime.

10 Signs of Better Security

The Coalition is working with Iraqis to improve internal security throughout the country. While the security situation is improving, dangerous remnants of the former regime and others continue to target progress and success.

1. New Iraqi army and police forces are being recruited, trained, and equipped. Some 1,200 Iraqis will be trained this year for the new Iraqi army, and in two years, 40,000 army recruits will be trained.
2. Fifty-eight of 89 Iraqi cities have hired police forces. In total, 34,000 Iraqis are employed in patrolling the streets of their country, and of these, 30,000 Iraqis are currently patrolling with coalition forces.
3. More than 8,200 tons of ammunition, thousands of AK-47s, grenades, and other weapons have been seized throughout Iraq—much of which was stored by the Hussein regime in hospitals, schools, and mosques.
4. The CPA has hired more than 11,000 Iraqis to guard key facilities around the country.
5. Coalition forces, with information from an Iraqi, conducted operations that led to the deaths of Uday and Qusay Hussein following their refusal to surrender. To date, 37 of the top 55 most wanted Iraqis have been captured or killed. With the deaths of Uday and Qusay, more and more Iraqis are freed from their fear and are volunteering their services and information.
6. Coalition forces continue to take the offensive against the remnants of the Ba'athist regime who are targeting the sites and symbols of reconstruction and stabilization successes.
7. An Iraqi Civil Defense Force will help U.S. and Coalition forces in rooting out Saddam loyalists and criminal gangs who have been attacking military forces and obstructing reconstruction efforts. Four thousand Iraqi militiamen will be trained by U.S. troops over the next eight weeks.

8. In Basra, 500 river police have been patrolling since June 19.

9. Some 148,000 U.S. service members and more than 13,000 Coalition troops from 19 countries are serving in Iraq.

10. Most of Iraq is calm and progress on the road to democracy and freedom not experienced in decades continues. Only in isolated areas are there still attacks.

10 Signs of Better Infrastructure and Basic Services

1. Electricity: Electricity is now more equitably distributed and more stable, instead of, as during Saddam Hussein's rule, being supplied to Baghdad at the expense of the rest of the country. For the rest of 2003, $294 million is budgeted to improve electrical systems.

2. Water Systems: Water supply in many areas is now at pre-conflict levels. Over 2,000 repairs have been made to 143 water networks, and water quality sampling has restarted. There are plans to add 450 million liters of capacity to Baghdad's system.

3. Healthcare: Iraqi hospitals are up and running, and healthcare, previously available only for Ba'athist elite, is now available to all Iraqis. Drugs are being supplied to hospitals and clinics, and medical worker salaries are being paid regularly, ensuring employees attend work. Vaccinations are available across the country, and anti-malarial spraying will take place this autumn.

4. Returning Refugees: Refugees began returning from Saudi Arabia and the United Arab Emirates. UNHCR and the Coalition are working together to ensure that groups of refugees in Jordan and Iran can return to Iraq safely and comfortably in the near future.

5. Revitalizing of Oil Production and Distribution: Repairs and modernizations are being made to the antiquated and neglected oil production and distribution systems. Oil will provide the future wealth of the country but was severely misappropriated by the former regime.

6. Police: There are 6,000 police on the streets of Baghdad and 34 out of 60 police stations are currently operational. Throughout Iraq, there are some 30,000 police patrolling the streets.

7. Road Repairs: Emergency road repairs, underway throughout Iraq now, will employ even more Iraqis in the coming weeks.

8. Airports: The Baghdad and Basra airports are ready to open, and the airport in Basra is expected to begin commercial operations in August. Several airlines are likely to start regular air service to Iraq.

9. Major Bridges: $4.3 million has been provided to repair the Tikrit Bridge; $4.4 million to rebuild the Al Mat Bridge; and $3.2 million to rebuild the Khazir Bridge.

10. Port at Umm Qasr: The port at Umm Qasr is open and functioning again, and customs and port authority agents are being trained.

10 Signs of Democracy

1. A 25-member national Governing Council includes three women and Kurdish, Sunni, Christian, Turkmen, and Shi'ia representatives. The establishment of this body is a first and important move toward Iraqi self-government.

2. The Governing Council is creating a Preparatory Commission to write a constitution. After a constitution is approved, elections will lead to a fully sovereign Iraqi government.

3. There are municipal councils in all major cities and 85 percent of towns, enabling Iraqis to take responsibility for management of local matters like healthcare, water, and electricity.

4. Provisional councils have been formed in Najaf, Al Anbar, and Basra.

5. The Baghdad City Advisory Council was inaugurated on July 7, 2003. Its 37 members were selected by

members of the city's nine district councils, who themselves were selected by Baghdad citizens in 88 neighborhoods throughout the city.

6. Local governance councils are robust in Basra and Umm Qasr, helping to identify areas for immediate humanitarian and reconstruction assistance.

7. The Office of Human Rights and Transitional Justice is working to locate missing persons, investigate, analyze, and exhume mass graves, archive past human rights abuses and promote civic education/public awareness about human rights.

8. To facilitate voluntary resolutions of property claims, the Property Reconciliation Facility is being created.

9. The Coalition is helping fund and train Iraqis wanting to create their own non-governmental organizations. These new NGOs include public policy think tanks and an association of former political prisoners.

10. More than 150 newspapers are now published in Iraq offering Iraqis access to many different kinds of information. Foreign publications, radio, and television broadcasts are also available.

10 Improvements in the Lives of Iraqi Children

1. A "back to school" campaign delivered 1,500 kits with book bags, notebooks, pens and pencils that helped 120,000 students in Baghdad return to their classrooms in May 2003. In preparation for the new school year, 1.2 million kits for secondary school students and 4,000 kits for their schools including desks, chairs, blackboards, and bookshelves are arriving in Iraq.

2. Malnutrition contributed to high mortality rates in Iraq during Saddam's rule. The food aid for Iraq has continued to supply the public distribution system and has allowed the majority of Iraqis access to food rations. On July 15, the World Food Program reported that nearly 1.5 million metric tons of food, or more

162

than the three months supply required to keep the distribution system operating, have been dispatched to Iraq. An additional 2.2 million metric tons of food will arrive by the end of October. These steps will contribute to reversing malnutrition.

3. To date, 22.3 million doses of measles, tuberculosis, hepatitis B, diphtheria, whooping cough, tetanus, and polio vaccines have been provided, enough to vaccinate 4.2 million children.

4. Nearly all Iraqi children have finished their exams from last year and are ready to start a new school year in the fall. All universities are reopened.

5. A $53 million program to rehabilitate more than 100 schools and clinics is underway. In the southern region, more than 50 schools are in various stages of rehabilitation. More than 600 schools will be in "like new" condition in time for the beginning of classes.

6. Five million revised math and science textbooks will be ready before the start of the school year.

7. Saddam Hussein's rhetoric is being removed from Iraqi schoolchildren's textbooks. In the words of Dunia Nabel, a teacher in Baghdad: "We want flowers and springtime in the texts, not rifles and tanks." (*Chicago Tribune*, July 31, 2003).

8. Ten delivery rooms in hospitals and primary healthcare centers in Basra have been rehabilitated and stocked with essential drugs and medical supplies.

9. The juvenile institution for children that was the subject of reports of abuse and appalling conditions under Saddam Hussein has been replaced by a project run by UNICEF and NGOs. Seven orphanages have undergone major building renovations and training for staff.

10. Nearly 3,000 soccer balls were shipped on May 30 and another 60,000 balls on their way to Iraq through a private/public partnership and the U.S. soccer community.

10 Signs of Economic Renewal

1. A New Economy: A new Iraqi economy is being built on the principles of market economics, respect for the rule of law, and transparency.

2. Salaries: The CPA regularly pays salaries to those teachers, healthcare workers, soldiers, police, and other public sector employees who have returned to work. Payments of pensions and other emergency payments have also helped to avert a humanitarian crisis. Teachers' salaries, and other key employees' salaries, have increased four-fold over their pay under Saddam Hussein. Some 39,000 electrical workers are back at work. Other sectors show similar encouraging signs.

3. Commerce: The marketplace in Baghdad has many goods that were previously unavailable because of sanctions or because they were forbidden under the previous regime. Items such as satellite dishes are now readily available to Iraqis.

4. Banks: Banks are open in Baghdad. The CPA is working with Iraqis outside of Baghdad to open banks across the country as soon as possible. In addition, international interest in establishing an Iraqi trade bank has been strong, and proposals from foreign banks are under review for creating this trade facility.

5. Food: The CPA has purchased the upcoming wheat and barley crops, helping to meet the country's food needs while supporting farmers. These crops include over 600,000 metric tons of Iraqi wheat and more than 300,000 metric tons of Iraqi barley.

6. Loans for Entrepreneurs: A micro-credit facility is now being set up in the South. Credit facilities for the rest of the country are also planned. Iraq's two major banks will start making small and medium sized business loans to help Iraqi entrepreneurs restart their businesses.

7. Currency: A unified currency for Iraq has been announced. The exchange of old banknotes for new ones is set to begin October 15.

8. Iraqis' Savings: The dinar has maintained its value against the dollar, preserving the dinar-dominated savings of Iraqi citizens.
9. Natural Resources: Oil production is increasing, with daily production of crude averaging 1 million barrels in recent days.
10. Budget: The budget for the last six months of 2003 is now being executed, and the 2004 budget formulation process has begun. Of the 2003 budget, more than $400 million has been released to Ministries in July and August alone. The 2004 budget process, to be run by Iraqis, will target the most important priorities for the country's reconstruction and build on the spending commitments of the budget for the last six months of 2003.

10 Examples of International Support for the Renewal of Iraq

1. The United Nations Secretary General Kofi Annan said of the Iraqi Governing Council: "[The Council's] formation is an important first step towards the full restoration of Iraqi sovereignty." The UN is supporting the renewal of Iraq through the Oil for Food program, and by providing humanitarian assistance, promoting human rights, and assisting the Iraqi Governing Council in rejoining the international community.
2. The United Nations Security Council passed, without opposition, Resolution 1483, lifting sanctions against the Iraqi regime.
3. The top 12 financial supporters for the renewal of Iraq are (in descending order): the United States, United Kingdom, Canada, Japan, Australia, Germany, Norway, Denmark, United Arab Emirates, Saudi Arabia, Spain, and Kuwait.
4. The UN reports that its total humanitarian assistance for the people of Iraq is $2.2 billion, of which $1.2 billion is pledged or contributed from the international

community and $1 billion is funded through the Oil for Food program.

5. In addition, several countries have pledged $800 million to UN programs. Nearly three dozen countries have made pledges or contributions to the renewal of Iraq.

6. There are now 34 foreign missions in Baghdad. Kuwait has reestablished relations with Iraq.

7. International pledges for reconstruction assistance are almost $3 billion, and an international conference to discuss additional funding for Iraq is scheduled for the fall.

8. More than 45 countries have offered military forces. The United Kingdom and Poland are each leading multinational divisions.

9. Numerous countries have contributed to the Coalition by providing basing and fly-over rights, as well as logistical support.

10. A total of 19 countries providing more than 13,000 troops in Iraq are supporting Operation Iraqi Freedom, and 14 countries are committed to deploying additional troops.

10 Signs of Cultural Rebirth

1. Iraqi Olympic Committee is reconstituted without fear from Uday Hussein: The new President of the Free Iraq Olympic group said, "The Iraqi teams used to produce the champions of Asia in many sports. They have declined since the arrival of Uday. Now we want to rebuild them with the help of the international community."— Sharar Haydar, one of Uday Hussein's former torture victims, *The Guardian* (London), May 15, 2003.

2. The Baghdad symphony is performing, and their concerts are also being televised. The conductor of the symphony said, "We're trying to show the world that Iraqis have a great culture."—Hisham Sharaf, at a

performance of the Baghdad Symphony, Agence France Presse, June 12, 2003.

3. Theaters are quickly reopening. In the words of one filmmaker: "You cannot imagine what it means for us to be here on this national stage, where everything we stand for was forbidden. Now it is ours."—Oday Rashid, *Los Angeles Times*, May 5, 2003.

4. Religious rites are being reestablished. As one Iraqi said: "I can't express my feelings. All I feel is joy. This is the first time I've seen this (Shiite celebrations) for 30 years. Saddam forbade everything. He forced us underground."—Sami Abbas, a Shia at the holy shrine of Kadhimiy, *Washington Post*, April 16, 2003.

5. 150 newspapers on the streets of Baghdad help get out the news of a free Iraq. Ali Jabar is quoted as saying, "Every day I buy a different paper. I like them all." Says a newspaper editor: "We can't train staff fast enough. People are desperate here for a neutral free press after 30 years of a totalitarian state."—Saad al-Bazzaz, editor of the *Azzaman Daily* in Baghdad, *The Independent* (London), July 8, 2003.

6. Satellite dishes are the most popular items for sale in Baghdad. "I want to watch all of the world, all channels in the world. I want to watch freedom."—Mohammed al-Khayat, an Iraqi who just purchased his first satellite dish, *Baltimore Sun*, April 26, 2003.

7. Banned books are now available in the market. A teacher selling books in Baghdad said: "Before, so many books were forbidden—anything that didn't agree with the regime. Which means practically everything that was ever printed!"—Imad Saad, *Los Angeles Times*, May 3, 2003.

8. Artists are free to display their works and poets are free to write. As one poet said: "For decades, we were used to watching ourselves. Now you can think with words. But to talk loudly and to think loudly takes time. Freedom needs practice, and it takes practice to be

free."—Mohammed Thamer, *Washington Post*, April 22, 2003.

9. Education is being revitalized. As a member of Baghdad's city council pointed out, "We want to have a real education, to be a progressive country. Education is very important to the reconstruction of our society. If you want to civilize society, you must care about education."—Al Sa'ad Majid al Musowi, *Chicago Tribune*, July 31, 2003.

10. The Marshlands are being rehabilitated. In the words of one Iraqi, "We broke the dams when the Iraqi army left. We want to teach our children how to fish, how to move on the water again."—Qasim Shalgan Lafta, a former fisherman who helped restore the water to the Iraqi wetlands that Saddam had destroyed, *Chicago Tribune*, June 13, 2003.

10 Steps to Improve the Lives of Iraqi Women

1. The Coalition is working to ensure that women play an important role in all parts of the government.

2. Three Iraqi women who are members of the new Governing Council are fully engaged in promoting the involvement of women in Iraq's future.

3. An esteemed former female Iraqi judge in the Ministry of Justice is undertaking a review of laws, legal practices, and the legal profession in Iraq for ways to increase equality and participation of women.

4. The Ministry of Interior conducted an assessment of the former Iraqi Police Force in early April. This resulted in a requirement to target recruitment of women and their inclusion in training offered at all academies. The program will become a reality August 15 when the recruiting drive begins with women as one of the groups targeted for selection.

5. The Ministry of Labor and Social Affairs has adopted a policy of equal access to services and benefits for all those eligible, and this policy will ultimately expand

services as well as quality to larger numbers of Iraqis including women.

6. Iraqi women will have a role in the development of democracy and civil society. A senior administration official from the CPA Democracy and Governance team is conducting outreach activities to involve Iraqi women.

7. The Coalition team has held numerous meetings with Iraqi women from all walks of life to hear their concerns and to listen to their ideas for the future development of democracy in their country. In addition, the CPA has met with various women's groups and with international organizations regarding their ideas and efforts to meet the needs of Iraqi women.

8. The Coalition helped a group of Iraqi women conduct a conference July 9 that included workshops on the constitution and democracy, legal reform, education, health and social affairs, and economic and employment issues. More than 70 women attended, the majority of whom were Iraqi women.

9. Quotas restricting the entry of women into certain university courses have been raised or lifted altogether.

10. Iraqi women's organizations are being created to expand opportunities for women to improve their lives and those of their families.

10 Voices of Liberation

You can find more voices of liberation on the White House Web site, http://www.whitehouse.gov/liberation/.

1. "We want to have a real education, to be a progressive country. Education is very important to the reconstruction of our society. If you want to civilize society, you must care about education."—Al Sa'ad Majid al Musowi, a businessman on Baghdad's city council, *Chicago Tribune*, July 31, 2003.

2. "We have full freedom to print anything we want. The coalition doesn't interfere in our work but, of course,

we have our own red lines."—Ishtar el Yassiri, editor of the new satirical Iraqi newspaper *Habez Bouz, Financial Times* (London), July 31, 2003.

3. "The tension is reducing every day. We are seeing a change. People are starting to realize that the soldiers are not here to occupy Fallujah forever—they're here to help us rebuild."—Taha Bedawi, mayor of Fallujah, *Washington Post*, July 29, 2003.

4. "It's a chance to defend our country for our people. It's good to work with the American soldiers. They give us new training and a mutual respect."—Omar Abdullah, a recruit for Mosul's newly formed joint security group, Associated Press, July 29, 2003.

5. "I want to serve a new Iraq."—Shevin Majid, a former Kurdish fighter who is now a recruit in the Mosul joint security force, Associated Press, July 29, 2003.

6. "More and more businessmen are coming to Iraq. It is a rich country and the Iraqi market is enormous. All the world wants to come and do business here."— Captain Adel Khalaf, director of the port at Umm Qasr, Agence France Presse, July 27, 2003.

7. "For the first time I feel really free."—Latif Yahia, Uday's former double, after hearing of Uday's death, Agence France Presse, July 26, 2003.

8. "The Iraqi people have got rid of two of the biggest criminals in history. Their victims and the sons of their victims, who lived for 35 years under oppression, are feeling proud and happy."—Muwaffak al-Rubaiei, a member of the Iraqi Governing Council, Agence France Presse and Reuters, July 25, 2003.

9. "I couldn't show it to the people in the past because of the regime. Now I hang it up to show respect."—Abbas Fadel, who displays a picture of his brother, tortured and murdered by Saddam Hussein, Knight Ridder, July 24, 2003.

10. "I can see that the American soldiers are free. In our old army, we were always under pressure and strict

military orders. There was tough punishment."—Raad Mamoud, a former Iraqi soldier, *USA Today*, July 21, 2003.

[NOTE: Material from the White House Web site (http://www.whitehouse.gov/infocus/iraq/100days/part10.html). Reproduced with permission of the White House.]

Table of Contents, Previous Volumes in this Series

Volume One: Culture Clash/Media Demons

173

Volume Two: Trade Towers/War Clouds

Volume Three: Making War/Making Peace

Volume Four: In the Shadow of War

Notes on Contributors

Joseph F. Coates has consulted to 45 of the Fortune 100 companies, smaller firms, trade, professional, public interest groups, and government. He is the coauthor of four books and author of more than 300 articles and papers on the future. He serves on 11 editorial boards. See his Web site: www.josephcoates.com.

Terrance L. Furin, Ph.D., is an Assistant Professor of education at Saint Joseph's University in Philadelphia. Prior to this, he was a school superintendent for 22 years. As a high school teacher in the 1960s and '70s, he came to know the special gifts that youth bring to political conversations. E-mail can be sent to tfurin@sju.edu.

Ted Goertzel, Ph.D., is Professor of Sociology at Rutgers University in Camden, New Jersey. His most recent book is *Cradles of Eminence*, Second Edition, an update of a classic book on the childhoods of famous people first published by his parents in 1962. He has also published a biography of former Brazilian President Fernando Henrique Cardoso and many other books and articles that are available at http://crab.rutgers.edu/~goertzel.

Lane Jennings, Ph.D., is a writer and book reviewer for the World Future Society and Production Editor of the Society's abstract journal *Future Survey*. His e-mail address is lanejen@aol.com.

Benjamin Liebman, Ph.D., is an Assistant Professor of economics at Saint Joseph's University in Philadelphia. Ben received his Ph.D., from the University of Oregon in 2003, several years after earning his undergraduate degree in English from Oberlin College in Ohio. He lives outside Philadelphia with his wife Kashawna and his two-year old daughter Michaela.

Michael Marien is founder and editor of *Future Survey* (see Appendix One), published monthly by the World Future Society in Bethesda, Maryland, since 1979 (www.wfs.org). Marien holds a Ph.D. in social science from the Maxwell Graduate School of Citizenship and Public Affairs at Syracuse University.

Shumi Nagpal comes from a diplomatic family, has traveled to more than 20 countries, and speaks six languages. She heads the international enrollment department at Drexel University. She has lectured on multicultural issues to students locally and internationally, and is a mother of four. She can be reached at sm48@drexel.edu.

Alexander G. Nikolaev, Ph.D., is an Assistant Professor of communication at Drexel University in Philadelphia. He earned his doctorate from the Florida State University where he also taught for four years. His areas of research interest and expertise include such fields as public relations; political communication; organizational communication; international communication; international news coverage; and discourse analysis. He authored several articles in these areas in trade and scholarly journals as well as several essays in the series *Defeating Terrorism/Developing Dreams: Beyond 9/11 and the Iraq War*. He also has years of practical work experience in the fields of journalism and public relations in both the United States and Eastern Europe. His current research focuses on international political rhetoric, international news coverage, and transformations and applications of the two-level-game theory.

Jim Pinto was formerly founder and CEO of a high-technology company based in San Diego, California. He is now a technology futurist, angel investor, speaker, writer, commentator, and consultant. His recent book *Automation Unplugged* was published by ISA. He invites your feedback, ideas, suggestions, and encouragement. Visit his Web site: www.JimPinto.com; or e-mail: jim@jimpinto.com.

Michael Radu, Ph.D., is cochairman of the Foreign Policy Research Institute's Center on Terrorism, counterterrorism, and Homeland Security (www.fpri.org). For the past 20 years, he has specialized in the study of terrorist groups worldwide.

Chris Seiple is the president of the Institute for Global Engagement, an international religious freedom "think tank with legs." Web site: http://www.globalengagement.org.

Peter Shaw is a high school history teacher currently substitute teaching in Vancouver, Washington. He is also an activist for Jobs with Justice and the Portland Central America Solidarity Committee (PCASC) and occasionally does photography and journalism for both organizations. He enjoys playing guitar and basketball as well as gardening and talking with his parents. He can be reached at pwshaw@yahoo.com.

Arthur B. Shostak, Ph.D., (Editor) has retired from being a Professor of Sociology since 1967 at Drexel University, Department of Culture and Communication, Philadelphia, PA 19104 (shostaka@drexel.edu). Since he began college teaching in 1961 he has specialized in trying to apply sociology to real-time problems ("challenges") and in shaping and communicating long-range forecasts. He has written, edited, and coedited 30 books and more than 150 articles. He especially recommends to readers of this volume his 2003 edited collection, *Viable Utopian Ideas: Shaping a Better World* (M.E. Sharpe).

R. Dean Wright, Ph.D., is the Ellis and Nelle Levitt Professor of Sociology at Drake University in Des Moines, Iowa. He is the past president of the Midwest Sociological Society, chair of the Iowa Criminal and Juvenile Justice Council, chair of the Salvation Army Board of Greater Des Moines, and Executive Director of Iowa Campus Compact. His research interest is in poverty, homelessness, and crime. He and his coauthor, William Du Bois, have published *Applying Sociology: Making a Better World* (2001). E-mail: dean.wright@drake.edu.

Robert Zaller, Ph.D., is Professor of History at Drexel University. He is the author of *The Parliament of 1621: A Study in Constitutional Conflict* and *Europe in Transition, 1660–1815*, and coauthor of *Civilizations of the World* and *Civilizations of the West*, among other works. He is a Fellow of the Royal Historical Society.

Index

185

Index

Index

Rule-of-law, 94
Rumsfeld, Doctrine, 86–88

Sadr, Sheik al-, 94–95
Sadr, Mohammed Sadiq al-, 94–95
Saudi Arabia, 120, 126, 141
Schneier, Bruce, 154–155
Schram, Martin, 141–142
"The Second Nuclear Age"
    (Keller), 140–141
Secrecy, bureaucratic, 61
Security
    homeland, 142–143, 154–155
    and religion, 94–95
    signs of better, 157, 159–160
    trade-offs for, 154–155
Seiple, Chris
    biographical information, 182
    "Religion and the New Global
        Counterinsurgency," 84–96
Seixas, Moses, 91
Shaw, Peter
    biographical information, 182
    "Living History, Making
        History, and Listening to
        Stories," 97–106
Shia Hezbollah, Lebanese, 81,
    139
Shostak, Arthur B. (editor)
    biographical information, 182
    "Introduction," 21–25
Simon, Paul, 108, 112–113
Singer, P.W., 151–153
Small Wars Manual, 89
Social studies, absence of, 111
Sokoloff, Harris, 112
"Sounds of Silence" (song), 108
Speech, freedom of, 46–47
Stanley, Timothy J., 111
Steinbruner, John D., 137–138
Stern, Jessica, 138–140
Strategies, 90–91
Student antiwar protests in
    United States, 109
Suicide bombers, 81–83
Sunni triangle, 31

Sunnis, 30, 89, 95, 139
Sweet Water Canal, 72
Symphony, Baghdad, 166–167
Syria, 30, 140–141

Tax cuts, cost of, 39
Technology investments, 150
Terrorism, 41, 138–140,
    147–148, 149
    See also War on Terrorism
    global war on, 85–86, 127–133
*Terrorism, Freedom, and Security:
    Winning Without War*
    (Heymann), 147–148
Time magazine, 35
Tito, Joseph Broz, 30–31
Tolerance, 91
Truman, Harry, 116
Truth, universality of, 58–59

The Ultimate Terrorists (Stern),
    138
UN (United Nations), 38–39,
    47, 58, 60, 101–102
*Understanding Terrorism:
    Challenges, Perspectives, and
    Issues* (Martin), 148–149
Unilateralism of United States,
    141
United Nations (UN), 38–39,
    47, 58, 60, 101–102
United States
    antagonism to, 30
    budget deficit, 39
    Constitution of, 60, 110,
        131–132
    imperialism of, 91–96,
        136–137, 144–145
    imposing values on others,
        49–50
    oil production and, 123–124
    policies of, 140, 144–145
    self-righteousness of, 59–60,
        64
    UN and, 38–39
    world opinion of, 58, 105

Index